Moonbit

Figure 1. Hieronymus Bosch, *Ship of Fools* (1490–1500)

First published in 2019 by punctum books, Earth, Milky Way.
https://punctumbooks.com

ISBN-13: 978-1-950192-33-5 (print)
ISBN-13: 978-1-950192-34-2 (ePDF)

DOI: 10.21983/P3.0260.1.00

LCCN: 9781950192335
Library of Congress Cataloging Data is available from the Library of Congress

Book design: Vincent W.J. van Gerven Oei
Cover image: Apollo 11 Mission image – CSM over the Sea of Tranquility (AS11-37-5448, July 20, 1969) – The Apollo 11 Command and Service Modules (CSM) (tiny dot near quarter-sized crater, center), with astronaut Michael Collins, command module pilot, aboard. The view overlooking the western Sea of Tranquility was photographed from the Lunar Module (LM). Astronauts Neil A. Armstrong, commander, and Edwin E. Aldrin Jr., lunar module pilot, manned the LM and made their historic lunar landing on July 20, 1969. Coordinates of the center of the terrain in the photograph are 18.5 degrees longitude and .5 degrees north latitude.

MOONBIT

James E. Dobson
Rena J. Mosteirin

Contents

R00000 – Introduction   13

R00001 – Code Hermeneutics   23

R00002 – The AGC and Computing in the 1960s   41

Moonbit: Erasure Poems Derived from Apollo 11 Source Code   61

    Part One: Comanche   63

    Comanche   65
    Pinball Noun Tables   66
    Of Next Burn   67
    Alarm and Abort   68
    To Load into Smode   69
    Waitlist   70
    Goneby   71
    Fresh Start   72
    Star Tables   73
    Time of Free Fall   75
    Jet Selection Logic   77
    Lunar and Solar Ephemerides Subroutines   78
    Erasable Assignments   79
    Erasable Assignments 2.0   80
    Antenna   82

    Part Two: 64 Found Bits (8 poems made of 8 octets of erasure)   83

ANGLFIND   85
CM_BODY_ATTITUDE   87
CONIC_SUBROUTINES   89
STABLE_ORBIT   91
PLANETARY INERTIAL ORIENTATION   93
P11   95
INTERPRETER   97
FILE OF THE SAME NAME   99

Part Three: Moonbit: The 64 Bit Poem Breakdown   101

    Anglfind   103
    Body Attitude   104
    Conic Subroutines   105
    Stable Orbit   107
    Planetary Inertial Orientation   108
    P11   109
    Interpreter   111
    File of the Same Name   113

R00003 — Code Poetics   115

R00004 — Cold War Code and the Doubled Discourse of Programming   127

Bibliography   141

Acknowledgments

We would like to thank Don Eyles, who answered several questions via email and who generously showed us his printed copy of the AGC code and parts of the hardware at a reading from *Sunburst and Luminary* at the MIT Museum in March of 2018.

We presented material from this book at two conferences, HaPoP in March of 2018 at University of Oxford and SIGCIS/SHOT in November 2018 in St. Louis, Missouri. We would like to thank the organizers, participants, and audience members at these two events for including us and for many very helpful questions and suggestions.

Ronald S. Burkey, creator of the *Virtual AGC project,* curator of a wealth of information about the Apollo computers, and author of numerous software components, including yaYUL and yaAGC, answered several questions and supplied one of the high-resolution scanned images included in this book. Without Ron's work and ongoing maintenance and stewardship, the AGC code would remain locked in paper and the subject of only historical inquiry. Thank you also to Jim Lawton for his work on the iBiblio website and archive.

Rena J. Mosteirin wishes to express her gratitude to her mentors from the Bennington Writing Seminars, where she developed many of the ideas that came to fruition in this book: Mark Wunderlich, April Bernard, Major Jackson, and Carmen Giménez-Smith.

We have been consistently inspired by the work that punctum books makes possible and we offer our warmest thanks to Eileen Joy and Vincent W.J. van Gerven Oei.

Dedicated to William W. Cook, teacher and poet.

R00000

Introduction

"I dare to imagine the general public learning how to write code. I do not mean that knowledge of programming should be elevated to the ranks of the other subjects that form basic literacy: languages, literature, history, psychology, sociology, economics, the basics of science and mathematics. I mean it the other way around. What I hope is that those with knowledge of humanities will break into the closed society where code gets written: invade it."
—Ellen Ullman, *Life in Code*

This collaboratively authored work, much like the object that has inspired it, is nonlinear and modular. It has been compiled together from several smaller component parts. We invite you to read this book accordingly. We have provided a series of experimental readings – just a few of what we believe to be the numerous explorations of the creative possibilities found within the confines of a rigidly constructed formal language that was once used to facilitate the breaking of existing spatial boundaries. We intend each section to expose new horizons of interpretation and exploration for understanding the poetics of code.

Throughout this book, we seek to show that software, or more specifically computer code, in excess of its bare functionality or its use value as an instrument to achieve some planned and programmed goal, also has numerous aesthetic properties and creative features. The aesthetic features of computer code – often characterized by a rigidly formal, restricted syntax, and numerous paralinguistic dimensions – sometimes have a supplemental character; they appear, at times, almost ornamental in their sheer excess beyond the functional elements and programmed goals. At other times, these features are an intrinsic and necessary part of the code. We believe that these special properties of computer code make possible imaginative uses or misuses by its human programmers and that these properties and features justify our exuberant readings, misreadings, translations, and appropriations.

At its base, this book is a poetic and philosophical meditation on the idea of computer code and the affordances and limitations of a language that is machine-oriented yet human-authored. The ordered instructions of this technological language work overtime to keep at bay the disorder of the world and the imprecision found in human language and thought. At the same time, this book is also a work of cultural analysis that examines what we will show to be the intersections of several distinct discourses that are all registered in this now obsolete and obscure computer language: the dreams and aspirations of 1960s computer and space science, the Cold War ideologies that enabled these technologies, the knowledge gained from the application of these technologies that was then used to advance and exercise imperial military power, and the traces of a counter-cultural language that emerged to supplement and at times resist components of the sparse, stripped-down syntax of these other discourses. Recovering, uncovering, and decoding these imbricated discourses requires the resources of multiple fields and approaches — methods both specialized and radically undisciplined.

Together, we take up a fascinating and now monumentally important historical source text for our critical and creative readings: the source code for the guidance computer that powered both the command and lunar modules for the Apollo Project, and specifically the version or edition of the code as used in the legendary Apollo 11 mission from July 16 to July 24 1969. This book appears during the fiftieth anniversary of this historic flight and we want to use this moment and our work to commemorate and critique this scientific and cultural event. This code was one of the technologies that made space travel possible; it would not be wrong to say that we wrote our way to the Moon. The Apollo Project, with its grand ambitions and aims, has inspired countless students, scientists, and engineers to dream big, to find and follow their vocations into the sciences and the arts, and to launch their own large-scale imaginative projects. Yet one of the most crucial newly developed technologies that enabled the astronauts to land on and return from the Moon, the digital computer that provided these astronauts with guidance data and assisted in the control of the Lunar and Command Module, has remained somewhat cloaked in obscurity. Unavailable and un-interpretable to the larger public, the text of the code powering this revo-lutionary computer remained locked within what we might call its base or bare functionality.

Each section of this book highlights and illuminates different aspects and dimensions of the Apollo Guidance Computer (AGC) code and the cultur-al moment that enabled its construction. We are producing code commen-tary — remarking and remixing the code. We intend no single account of the code to be definitive; our purpose in presenting critical commentaries alongside poetry is to interrupt the desire to fix and re-instrumentalize our source text. Instrumentalization, in part, involves the flattening of a tech-nology into a mere tool and the privileging of what we might term the an-thropological account of a technology as a means by which to accomplish some goal. In reading an object that one might assume to be the province of one culture through the tools and methodologies of another, we want to show that this division, the now entrenched separation of the sciences and the humanities, itself has already been called into question by the invention of code.[1] Proceeding from here, we provide wide ranging readings, responses, and interpretations of the code that we believe will aid our readers in thinking broadly about exploration, collaboration, and computation. Moonbit will not get you to the Moon, but seeks to re-claim the text that did this, as a site for artistic exploration.

It is in this spirit that we write this book as a collaborative project. Inspired by the collective work of over four hundred programmers, writers, engineers, project managers, and others who worked on the various Apollo 11 digital computer systems – both hardware and software – not to mention the hundreds of thousands participating in the larger 1960s space program itself, we "compiled" this book from a critical reading and what could be called a deformation of its source text into a collection of poems and expansive commentary. We would like to think of this project as a set of remarks – here we use remarks in order to riff on the term for the existing formalized commentary supplied by the original authors of the code and included within the body of the code – on the code that frame and elaborate the meaning of the code at its point of origin in 1969, its longer historical context of the development of computing and scientific exploration, and the code's meaning for our present moment.

The authors of another study and exploration of "old" and obsolete code, *10 PRINT CHR$(205.5+RND(1)); : GOTO 10*, faced a much larger task than ours at present: convincing their readers that their singular titular line of BASIC code for the Commodore 64, a popular home computer produced during the 1980s, was an important cultural artifact and one worth engaging with in the present and that their interpretations and readings had value for software studies. They write:

The subject of this book – a one-line program for a thirty-year-old microcomputer – may strike some as unusual and esoteric at best, indulgent and perverse at worst. But this treatment of *10 PRINT* was undertaken to offer lessons for the study of digital media more broadly. If they

---

1   In "New Methods for Humanities Research," his 2005 Lyman Award Lecture, prominent digital humanities scholar John Unsworth cites Bill Wulf, a former president of the National Academy of Engineering, as arguing that "computer science should really be considered one of the humanities, since the humanities deal with artifacts produced by human beings, and computers (and their software) are artifacts produced by human beings," http://people.virginia.edu/~jmu2m/lyman.htm.

prove persuasive, these arguments will have implications for the interpretation of software of all kinds.[2]

The examination of obsolete code, whether written, modified, and used by hundreds of thousands of hobbyist home computer owners or developed in secret for the US nationalist project of space exploration, brings elements of the past into the present and reveals how this obscure computational past might, to riff on William Faulkner, not even be past. We believe that the AGC code is of as much historical and cultural interest, if not more, as the memoirs, recordings, and documents that serve to record and shape our understanding of the inception and development of the US space program.

Source code appears throughout this book, sometimes with extensive commentary that draws out the implications, assumptions, and desires of the authors, and other times lines of code appear as suggestions or provocations. We do not expect the reader to be familiar with the specific language used or to have studied computer science. We present code as an interpretable object. This is because this particular code text, while restricted to the confines of the fixed format dictated by 1960s coding standards and requirements, contains a rich set of meta-commentary that explains as it codifies – that attempts to account, in a series of remarks, for the many decisions made and choices selected within the code. Code, it might surprise you to learn, is not written just for a computer; code, as we will show, has many audiences and can be shaped into several different forms. Code is not just what is executed by the computer, but a language, a discourse, with creative and functional possibilities. Contrary to the common perception of programming, code is not just a set of instructions, it is not just math. Even in the earliest and simplest of computer languages, written code is frequently imaginative and has the capacity to be wildly playful. Code contains within it a poetics of its very own. There is an aesthetics to be found within the construction of code but these aesthetic features sometimes exceed their functional value. We believe the AGC code to be truly remarkable code.

This book, in part, seeks to provide an introduction to the theory and practice of critical code studies. We seek to outline a more capacious version of critical code studies that takes up all manner of imaginative decodings and recodings of our object of analysis. In introducing some of the

---

2   Nick Montfort et al., *10 PRINT CHR$(205.5+RND(1)); : GOTO 10* (Cambridge: MIT Press, 2013), 5.

major existing approaches to the study of code and culture, we attempt to provide multiple readings of the source code along with an explanation and theorization of the way in which the Apollo Guidance Computer code works, as both a computational and a cultural text. We tend, however, to privilege the cultural rather than technical meanings of the code as we unpack, deform, and explicate. There are a number of existing accounts of the AGC hardware and software and while we will explore some of the functional purposes of this "antique" code, we are finally more interested in the way in which the code can become meaningful to its human readers. This is to say that we believe the code makes and contains interesting cultural commentary that we can read in relation to the historical moment in which the code was developed and used.

We draw out buried meaning and recode what was punched out through several interpretive and creative methods, including erasure. The AGC code provides rich source material that is about motion as much as it is about communication — complete with scatological jokes in the commentary. This code put people on the Moon and continues to inspire discovery. Erasure poetry, like the source language that it borrows from, offers itself as a way to memorialize or monumentalize while also making something new. The erasure method begins with a complete source text — really any sort of object — and removes much of it, creating a new text, a poem entirely wrought from some other primary textual source. Jen Bervin's *Nets* takes Shakespeare's sonnets as its source and erases most of the words, carving entirely new poems out of canonical literature. In contrast, Tom Phillips, in his art book *A Humument*, takes an unknown Victorian novel, *A Human Document* by W.H. Mallock, and erases most of it. Phillips makes each page into an original work of art, with only a few of Mallock's original words remaining. M. NourbeSe Phillip's *Zong!* makes a coherent cacophony of what remains from a massacre of one hundred and fifty slaves who were pushed off the slave ship Zong, so that the Zong's investors could re-coup what they lost in a failed venture in the form of insurance money. This case left behind a legal legacy of barely five hundred words. Phillip's book-length *Zong!* poem gives voice to those massacred people and distressingly, but correctly, offers the reader no consolation.[3]

3   Jen Bervin, *Nets* (Brooklyn: Ugly Duckling Presse, 2004); Tom Phillips, *A Humument* (London: Thames and Hudson, 1980); M. NourbeSe Philip, *Zong!* (Middletown: Wesleyan Univer-

Poems about space travel crave white space on the page. Here the white space represents the unknown cosmos or white light from the stars or perhaps the white face of the Moon itself. Erasure creates white spaces. Erasure creates room to breathe and space to think by finding holes within the source text or creating holes by erasing existing marks and larger textual structures. It navigates through these gaps, found or created, within the source text to bring something new into being. This debris may be of use. While there are computational methods for automatically producing erasure poetry, the poems in this book follow no program.[4] They are human responses to code written by other humans. As William W. Cook argues of Frederick Douglass's understanding of learning to write by "writing in the spaces left" in a source text: "In the spaces left he finds those uninscribed topoi necessary to his own creation. He writes a hand similar to, but not identical with, that of his model preparatory to taking full control of the text itself. Imitation and repetition lead here to creativity and liberation."[5] The AGC code itself contains multiple languages, multiple worlds. It contains subroutines to alter our orientation, to translate our coordinates, to alter its internal representation of space in terms of the Earth and the Moon. Erasure, for Brian McHale, engages in a cycle of "making and unmaking" that, in the case of James Merrill's work, "structure (and deconstruct) the world, or rather the *worlds* in the plural."[6] Applied to this multiple-worlded text at the limits of modernity, erasure reinserts the hand into the machine to liberate the poet and this text and in the process, destabilize the inscribed formal relations among the represented bodies.

The four hundred programmers and engineers working on the Apollo Guidance Computer were employed by the Draper Laboratories, later the MIT Instrumental Lab, in Cambridge, Massachusetts. The code was not developed in isolation; it builds upon prior knowledge and expertise, collabora-

sity Press, 2011).

4   See, for example, *The Deletionist* program created and theorized by Amaranth Borsuk, Jesper Juul, and Nick Montfort, "Opening a Worl in the World Wide Web: The Aesthetics and Poetics of Deletionism," *NMC: Media-N* 11, no. 1 (2015), http://median.newmediacaucus. org/the_aesthetics_of_erasure/opening-a-worl-in-the-world-wide-web-the-aesthetics-and-poetics-of-deletionism/.

5   William W. Cook, "Writing in the Spaces Left," *College Composition and Communication* 44, no. 1 (1993): 9–25, at 16.

6   Brian McHale, "Poetry under Erasure," in *Theory Into Poetry: New Approaches to the Lyric*, eds. Eva Müller-Zettelmann and Margarete Rubik (New York: Rodopi, 2005), 295.

tors within other organizations and departments, and the contributions of consultants and industry partners. These programmers and engineers developed the code with instructions from NASA, editing and debugging from Cambridge, while astronauts departed from Earth with their code, their creation, within the lunar and control modules.

The advent of the digital computers placed in the Apollo Lunar Module marked an incredibly important development in the history of digital computing and space flight. In the past few years there has been an increasing amount of interest in these systems and the people behind the development of this early code. Images of the printed code were scanned and uploaded to the information sharing site iBiblio and optical character recognition (OCR) software (along with some manual editing) was used to render these images of printed text legible in digital form. The archives of the code enabled hobbyists and space enthusiasts to explore and play with the AGC code but it remained difficult for browsers to understand the larger code project in its entirety until the text of the code was made available in a new form. It was, then, in 2016 that an intern at MIT uploaded the AGC code to the code repository Github, enabling global and easy access to the code along with the collaborative editing, commentary, and revision tracking system provided by the site. In the process of moving the code into Github, the code was segmented into separate files and presented in a form that would work with the Github conventions for displaying code, including the transformation of certain code features that formerly belonged in fixed positions into a contemporary, less structured form.

While the conversion of the AGC code into Github drew our attention to this code, our primary driver for exploring the code was the growing attention to the work of one particular MIT Instrumental Lab staff member that coincided with the Github "publication" of the Apollo code. In "compiling" our readings and responses into this book we seek, above all, to recognize and acknowledge the contributions of Margaret Hamilton, lead programmer on the Apollo Guidance Computer project. Hamilton was one of the few women working in the nascent field of computer engineering and the only female senior staff member. In November 2016, President Obama awarded Margaret Hamilton the Presidential Medal of Freedom. In his citation, Obama wrote of her many contributions, all of which were first imagined and explored in the text of the AGC code examined by this book: "Hamilton contributed to concepts of asynchronous software, priority scheduling and priority displays, and human-in-the-loop decision capability, which set the foundation for modern, ultra-reliable software design and engineering."[7] Hamilton's work on the Apollo project and that of many others helped to establish the field of software engineering and legitimized new discursive practices. Her work and imagination inspires our own flights of fancy as we produce numerous readings of the code that she committed to the Apollo Project.

7   President Barack Obama's citation reads as follows: "Margaret H. Hamilton led the team that created the on-board flight software for NASA's Apollo command modules and lunar modules. A mathematician and computer scientist who started her own software company, Hamilton contributed to concepts of asynchronous software, priority scheduling and priority displays, and human-in-the-loop decision capability, which set the foundation for modern, ultra-reliable software design and engineering." Office of the Press Secretary, "President Obama Names Recipients of the Presidential Medal of Freedom," *The White House*, November 16, 2016, https://obamawhitehouse.archives.gov/the-press-office/2016/11/16/president-obama-names-recipients-presidential-medal-freedom.

R00001

Code Hermeneutics

"The reasoning behind this part is involved."
—AGC Source Code

The Apollo Guidance Computer (AGC) code was primarily designed to be assembled and executed, not read and explored on the page. For those users of the several software emulators of the AGC, this is still an executable body of code. Yet this collection of code, like almost all code, is also a discursive object that registers and contains within its symbols, language, and self-understanding traces of its authorship, of its moment of production. Code, despite our ready assumptions of it as a set of concise, minimal, and utilitarian instructions, is an interpretable text. Code is a particular kind of polyvocal textual object. It is written for and addresses the particular software and hardware that define, to borrow a phrase from literary studies, what we might call its ideal reader. This reader is a particular platform with all its attendant affordances and limitations. Code, depending on the language and methods of abstraction, may very well run on other platforms without the work of porting, the translation of platform-specific code. Algorithms, of course, are generally platform-agnostic and can be reimplemented with relative ease. Code speaks, as it were, to multiple audiences and in multiple voices. There are multiple active discourses in much computer code and the AGC code provides contemporary readers with a particularly interesting site for examining the co-existence of these discourses.

But what sort of object is the AGC code? What sort of reading practices do we need to disentangle these discourses and interpret them? Should we consider code a text? Computer code, after all, is not – despite the way in which it is usually imagined by the public – constructed in ceaseless strings of 1s and 0s, but instead written using a standardized lexicon of textual signifiers, supplemented with some language-specific syntax. It is usually quite modular and organized into readable chunks with spacing and indentation used to enable comprehension. Code is almost always written and edited by humans. Almost every programming language borrows the major components of its syntax from a source "natural" language (this has been typically English) and programmers make logical and indeed creative and imaginative use of this language within both their code and their commentary.

Certainly, in the hands of cultural studies scholars, almost any object or action can be read as a discursively constructed text, from fashion to dance, from television programs to the Sony Walkman. Software, and especially computer code, can be understood as a cultural text because, as this book demonstrates, these texts are always constructed within the cultural constraints of the historical moment in which they were created and used. These constraints include, but are not limited to, the capabilities of particular hardware and supporting software libraries, major programming paradigms and languages, the so-called best practices of various programming communities, previously established methods and algorithms, the choices made by the few computer corporations that control the digital computer market, and the market available and constructed for the software product. For computational critic and theorist David Berry, code is a particularly important type of cultural text, because it simultaneously participates in several different registers. "Code," Berry writes, "needs to be approached in its multiplicity, that is, as a literature, a mechanism, a spatial form (organisation), and as a repository of social norms, values, patterns and processes."[1] Software, as the packaged and typically feature-frozen version of a selected configuration of code, touches more of these discourses and is under more of these constraints than the source code that typically remains hidden or obscured through the process by which it is compiled into machine executable software. But both software and source code register these frequently conflicting aspects of culture.

As a textually mediated mode of explanation and instruction written by a community of programmers and hackers, code shares much with other forms of textual expression, including literary texts. One powerful method by which we can examine the Apollo Guidance Computer code is through what literary scholar and theorist Caroline Levine calls the "new formalism." Levine's understanding of formalism is not limited just to the traditional aesthetic elements of formalism as used for decades within literary studies — the familiar practice of close reading that prompts the reader to cast her eye to language, lingering and dwelling on the appearance and significance of the words on the page — but also to a theoretically informed account of what Levine calls the "ordering principles." She uses this notion of ordering in her gloss of this updated or "new" formalist method that examines, broadly, "an arrangement of elements — an ordering, patterning, or shaping."[2] Levine's version of formalism pays close attention to the affordances of both literary, textual, and social structures — often these social structures are external to the text — and understands these various forms as not isolated phenomena but co-existing and in an informing re-

1   David M. Berry, *The Philosophy of Software Code and Mediation in the Digital Age* (New York: Palgrave, 2011), 36.
2   Caroline Levine, *Forms: Whole, Rhythm, Hierarchy, Network* (Princeton: Princeton University Press, 2015), 3.

lation to each other. This is to say that the aesthetic forms used within any particular text can have political implications and that political forms may contain within them an aesthetic element.

In the theoretically informed readings of the AGC code that follow, the question of relation between social and aesthetic forms will continually re-appear. In order to understand the AGC code and the multiple possible meanings produced and found within the code, we will have to shift the frame back and forth between different hermeneutical registers. This reading practice, like the code itself, might be thought of as modular and extensible.

The framework of the emergent field of critical code studies (CCS) pro-vides, through the tacit agreement of the different possible critical per-spectives, some possible methods through which we can frame and in-terpret the code. The close readings of code that follow will unpack and explain the purpose and aspirations of the displayed code segments. In so doing, the AGC software becomes visible as an important and readable cul-tural artifact and maybe even a work of art.

Computer software, cultural critic and theorist Lev Manovich tells us, is new media. Scholars working in the emergent field of software studies bring a range of critical resources, including ideological critique, formal analysis, and aesthetic criteria to bear on the design, construction, and everyday use of computer software. In several recent books, Manovich, one of the primary figures involved in the creation of software studies, asks us to take seriously the study of software, because software "mediates peo-ple's interfaces with media and other people."[3] More and more, our every-day interaction with both local and global news, weather reports, text, au-dio, and video messaging, music, movies, games, directions, and access to knowledge itself is fully mediated by an array of personal digital devices and the software that presents and shapes these services and experiences. Software, in short, is culture. While there are different kinds of software, and many different ways of studying software, Manovich examines the use of media software. He defends his decision to study the mostly commercial creative media software used by cultural workers by pointing to the large and mostly anonymous user base of these packages. He argues that he wants to analyze what he calls "mainstream cultural practices"[4] instead of the

3   Lev Manovich, *Software Takes Command* (New York: Bloomsbury, 2013), 29.
4   Ibid., 31.

exception: those developing software or those involved in modifying or tinkering with existing software. This approach is roughly analogous to the arguments made by some scholars of popular culture.

While Manovich focuses on the way in which users interact with software, in particular those software packages that are used to create and access new media, other scholars have begun investigating the internals of software, the code that enables software to produce these functions and interfaces. Critical code studies (CCS) is an emergent approach to the study of software and the code that makes up this software that originates in the critical approaches offered by the field of cultural studies. Proponents of CCS argue that we can read code as an object for critical analysis; in the way in which cultural studies describes images and objects as a text, code may also be understood as a text.

David M. Berry makes an important distinction between code and software. He uses the term code

> to refer to the textual and social practices of source code writing, testing, and distribution. In contrast 'software' (as prescriptive code) will refer to the object code, that is, code that has been compiled into an executable format, which includes final software products, such as operating systems, applications or fixed products of code such as Photoshop, Word and Excel.[5]

Berry's distinction depends on the division between executable, machine-readable software or compiled code and the source code that generates such software. This division is especially important to the commercial packages Berry mentions, Adobe's Photoshop and Microsoft's Word and Excel. These complex software packages are protected, controlled-access products. The code remains proprietary, a corporate secret, in order for the vendor — Adobe and Microsoft in the case of the packages mentioned by Berry — to sell access and, increasingly, automatically expiring subscriptions for the right to use the software products.

If, for David Berry, we should read code because code can give us insight into the software creation process, for Mark C. Marino, code is an important text in need of interrogation and critique because it offers a site for not

---

5   Berry, *The Philosophy of Software Code and Mediation in the Digital Age*, 64–65.

just the analysis of software culture, but for the larger project of cultural analysis. Marino argues that code is a layer of discourse – presumably he means by this that code exists in some relation to other forms of cultural discourse – loaded with significance. It is a particular kind of cultural text, one "with connotations that are in conversation with its functioning."[6] By this Marino means that the language that makes code work – the instructions, functions, and assignments – exceeds its instrumental value. Descriptive language – in his essay he highlights the naming of variables – makes something happen while also providing another type of meaning that is in excess of its functional value. While Marino's variable names are an example of natural language – typically they encode meaning within their abstraction as pointers to data by naming the pointer itself – within code, the particular programmatic choices including spacing and even the organization of the code are subject to this form of critique. Extending the scope of CCS beyond the formal readings of source code, Marino claims that critical code studies "explores existing programming paradigms, but it also questions the choices that were made, examining among other aspects the underlying assumptions, models of the world, and constraints (whether technological or social) that helped shape the code."[7] Scholars making use of CCS who work within cultural studies frame code as just another cultural, i.e., social text capable of revealing aspects of the culture that informed the writing of the code.

Because of the above issues involving the intersection of familiar or ordinary natural language appearing within code, the majority of debates within critical code studies and software studies has tended to discuss the philosophical nature of code and the relation between code, language, and writing. Alexander Galloway argues that code is different from writing, from language, because, in his account, code is a special type of language that he calls hyperlinguistic: "Code is a language, but a very special kind of language. *Code is the only language that is executable.*"[8] Galloway provocatively describes code as "the first language that actually does what it

---

6   Mark C. Marino, "Why We Must Read the Code: The Science Wars, Episode IV." In *Debates in the Digital Humanities*, eds. Matthew K. Gold and Lauren F. Klein (Minneapolis: University of Minnesota Press, 2016), 139.

7   Ibid., 140.

8   Alexander R. Galloway, *Protocol: How Control Exists after Decentralization* (Cambridge: MIT Press, 2004), 165.

says – it is a machine for converting meaning into action."[9] Language, one might argue contra Galloway's assertation, can do things, but he wants to make a distinction within code by introducing what he calls an executable state to his understanding of language:

> Code has a semantic meaning, but it also has an enactment of meaning. Thus, while natural languages such as English or Latin only have a legible state, code has both a legible and an executable state. In this way, code is the summation of language plus an executable metalayer that encapsulates that language.[10]

Code, of course, does not always do exactly what it says it will do – it is interpreted, by a compiler or interpreter, and the meaning of the code might not be the same meaning as the execution. Galloway concentrates mostly on compiled languages such as C and C++, in which the code is transformed into executable instructions by a compiler. Compilers (usually) create object code or bytecode, an essentially lower-level set of instructions that are optimized for system-specific hardware, including central processing units (CPUs) or virtualized systems (in the case of Java).[11] The notion of code as doing what it says becomes more complicated and less and less true as we add layers of abstraction and modularity. Because of Galloway's emphasis on compiled rather than interpreted languages, he tends to treat code as separable from its instruction. Interpreted languages are one step closer to programmers than the compiled languages critiqued by Galloway; the code is interpreted and executed by the interpreter as written, in its initial state. Interpreted languages are also subject to the critique of complex systems that will follow, but in general interpreted languages stay within what Galloway terms a legible state. Highly specialized and opaque code, as this book demonstrates, needs the supplement of natural language to make its meaning legible for human readers. This supplement renders the text of

9   Ibid., 165–66.
10   Ibid., 166.
11   The target, by which we mean an audience that must be addressed and included for compiled code. The target for most compiled "C" code on a modern Linux system is an optimized and dynamic stack of libraries. This target platform is described formally by the operating system as such: "ELF 64-bit LSB executable, x86-64, version 1 (SYSV), dynamically linked (uses shared libs), for GNU/Linux 2.6.18, stripped."

the AGC code a complex configuration of writing, a space-age entanglement of meaning making that invites the full resources of critical analysis to unpack and explore.

John Cayley, who helped inaugurate critical code studies and code poetics with his essay "The Code is not the Text (unless it is the Text)," helps us to think through this complex problem of the audience for code:

> If a codework text, however mutually contaminated, is read primarily as the language displayed on a screen then its address is simplified. It is addressed to a human reader who is implicitly asked to assimilate the code as part of natural language. This reading simplifies the intrinsically complex address of writing in programmable media. At the very least, for example, composed code is addressed to a processor, perhaps also addressed to specific human readers (those who are able to 'crack' or 'hack' it); while the text on the screen is simultaneously? asynchronously? addressed to human readers generally. Complexities of address should not be bracketed within a would-be creolized language of the new media utopia.[12]

Cayley is interested in a possible poetics of code and locates his investment in complicating the lines between code and text in his naming of the text of code "codework." Cayley positions his codework as addressed simultaneously to the machine and the human reader. Doing so enables him to resist the separation between what appears on a screen or device and the code that brings this digital appearance into being. For Cayley, the audience of code must always include the possibility of a human reader.

The question of audience and code legibility persists within CCS. N. Katherine Hayles follows Galloway's understanding of code as distinct from the natural language associated with writing because of its function and its primary audience. She argues that despite the possibility of human readers, code is written primarily for machines, for a computer:

> Although code originates with human writers and readers, once entered into the machine it has as its primary reader the machine itself. Before any screen display accessible to humans can be generated, the machine must first read the code and use its instructions to write messages hu-

---

12 John Cayley, "The Code Is Not the Text (Unless It Is the Text)," *Electronic Book Review*, September 10, 2002, http://www.electronicbookreview.com/thread/electropoetics/literal.

mans can read. Regardless of what humans think of a piece of code, the machine is the final arbiter of whether the code is intelligible.[13]

This difference is what enables her to construct a successive genealogy for "the three major systems for creating signification"[14]: "In the progression from speech to writing to code, each successor regime reinterprets the system(s) that came before, inscribing prior values into its own dynamics."[15] For Hayles, this process of reinterpretation does not necessarily obsolete the prior regime, but it does produce extensions and alterations that fundamentally exceed the capacity of the previous system to describe the new world inaugurated by the new regime. "One of Derrida's critical points," Hayles argues, "is that writing exceeds speech and cannot simply be conceptualized as speech's written form. Similarly, I will argue that code exceeds both writing and speech, having characteristics that appear in neither of these legacy systems."[16] Hayles's use of "legacy system" produces a shift, but it is not as dramatic of an obsoleting shift as it sounds — she calls speech and writing "vital partners on many levels of scale in the evolution of complexity."[17]

In a later work, Hayles doubles down on her argument that code must always be considered executable and that is always addressed to a specific interpretive community, the machine:

> If the transition from handwriting to typewriting introduced a tectonic shift in discourse networks, as Friedrich Kittler (1992) has argued, the couple of human institution and machine logic leads to specificities quite different in their effects from those mobilized by print. On the human side, the requirement to write executable code means that every command must be explicitly stated in the proper form. One must therefore be very clear about what one wants the machine to do.[18]

---

13 N. Katherine Hayles, *My Mother Was a Computer: Digital Subjects and Literary Texts* (Chicago: University of Chicago Press, 2005), 50.
14 Ibid., 39.
15 Ibid.
16 Ibid., 40.
17 Ibid., 55.
18 N. Katherine Hayles, *How We Think: Digital Media and Contemporary Technogenesis* (Chicago: University of Chicago Press, 2012), 42.

Despite the claims made by Galloway and Hayles, we cannot guarantee that the instructions will be executed as written because of the various levels and layers of abstraction involved in computing. The expected execution of even compiled code can be altered. Depending on the language and system used, there are multiple layers of interpretation and transformation that take place between the writer of code and the final execution of instructions. Modern computing systems are constructed from modular components, both software and hardware, and these components continually abstract any set of instructions.

This abstraction, which has been increasing throughout the past few decades, enables programmers to write shorter and simpler code – commonly used routines and procedures are frequently supplied by the operating system. Even if the programmer does not choose to use one of these supplied functions, many components of the software might be substituted by the operating system or by end users. These can be optimized for specific hardware (such as a device to offload certain operations to a Graphical Processing Unit or GPU) and software configurations. In the case of closed-source operating systems such as those supplied by Microsoft, these libraries contain well-known functions that enable software developers to write applications with a similar look and feel. Open-source platforms also make use of these types of libraries but also contain a large collection of libraries from other tools that contain these frequently used functions.

All of this is to say that the programmer cannot have any sort of guarantee that the code will be executed as written.[19] Code resembles more of wish than a command. Wendy Chun has provided one of the most pointed critiques of Galloway and Hayles's position. She takes issue with the reduction of software "to a recipe, a set of instructions" and argues that code is devious and crafty.[20] Chun demonstrates this by pointing to the layering involved in complex computer systems and the fact that because of the it-

19 Rita Raley complicates this understanding by asking us to consider the difference between code and computation. She does so by analyzing code that is not nor can never be executed and raises questions about the "function" of code specifically designed to fail or crash, in which its failure becomes precisely its successful function. See Rita Raley, "Code.surface || Code.depth," *Dichtung Digital* 36 (2006), http://www.dichtung-digital.org/2006/01/Raley/index.htm.
20 Wendy Hui Kyong Chun, *Programmed Visions: Software and Memory* (Cambridge: MIT Press, 2011), 21.

erative development cycle of software, "source code only becomes a source after the fact."[21] The "fact" of computation, in Chun's argument, requires the successful execution and testing of code. Execution makes and names the code that was executed "the source" for the executed code. The source code then might be said to retroactively become a re-source. Chun breaks with the normative understanding of code to expose what she calls the fetish logic of code:

> code as fetish thus underscores code as thing: code as a "dirty window pane," rather than as a window that leads us to the "source." Code as fetish emphasizes code as a set of relations, rather than as an enclosed object, and it highlights both the ambiguity and the specificity of code. Code points to, it indicates, something both specific and nebulous, both defined and indefinable. Code, again, is an abstraction that is haunted, a source that is a re-source, a source that renders the machinic — with its annoying specificities or "bugs" ghostly.[22]

Chun calls the belief that the only meaning of code could be what it does a form of "sourcery" that is in fact a fetish covering over the deviations between execution and code. The retroactive process that makes code a source after its "correct" execution leaves marks, leaves traces within the code — both within the functions and commands and within the natural language found within code comments.

Friedrich Kittler refers to the above referenced hierarchical layering of languages and instructions as a "postmodern Tower of Babel" that has produced a fog of interpretive confusion that covers over the gaps between instruction and execution — so much so that he argues that "we can simply no longer know what our writing is doing, and least of all when we are programming."[23] While some might take this confusing stack of instructions as provocation to examine computation, to turn to the task of translating the particularities of a language or machine-specific instructions into a common code, one for a universal computer, code (at least successfully executed code) is inscribed with the signs of being run through a configura-

---

21 Ibid., 24.
22 Ibid., 54.
23 Friedrich A. Kittler, *The Truth of the Technological World: Essays on the Genealogy of Presence*, trans. Erik Butler (Stanford: Stanford University Press, 2014), 221.

tion of hardware and software and these signs bear the traces of culture, of the programmer's membership within communities of practice. This is one that that we can be sure of when we talk about that type of writing called programming: when one writes code, one works with conventions. There might be only iterations of utterly conventional code to be found or perhaps when reading code we discover a range of imaginative and creative extensions, elaborations, and elegant appropriations. Programming might attempt to present itself as a form of wizardry or sorcery but it is ultimately the use of a communal language used by a certain type of desiring machine that is human, all too human.

The interpretive practices outlined above make the AGC code available to a wide range of contemporary readers. Potential readings include an antiquarian desire to take what might call a software archeological dig into this historical code or a culture critique that seeks to unpack the ways in which the functions, commands, and comments register the conditions that made the creation of this particular body of code possible. The esoteric and the aesthetic are combined and interleaved throughout the lines of this code and this combination invites reading with and against the grain. Historicizing, critiquing, and appreciating the language structuring the earlier years of programming and digital computers makes it possible to shift and ultimately shuttle our attention back and forth through the long history of computing, adding insight to both the past and the present of digital culture.

Reading Code

In order to help frame and make more concrete some of the objections and questions raised by the above arguments and their claims for the interpretation of the AGC code, we can turn to some contemporary and highly simplified examples of computer code. The following are lines of code written in a high-level interpreted programming language called Python. Python programs remain (generally) in textual or "source" form. These instructions are "read" and interpreted by the Python interpreter, itself written in the C programming language and compiled for a specific computing platform (for example, macOS running on the x86_64 CPU). This fragment of a program defines (def) a function named euclidean_distance. The function operates on two supplied input parameters (input1 and input2). Functions are the building blocks or components of well-designed larger programs. They enable more efficient and readable code by bundling together instructions that might be used multiple times within a single program. Functions, in Python and other programming languages, can be thought of as the addition of new instructions to the existing language resources. The euclidean_distance function calculates the "distance" between the two supplied parameters by taking the square root of the summed squared differences between the input objects supplied as the parameters.

```
def euclidean_distance(input1,input2):
    d = 0
    for i in range(len(input1)):
        d += (input1[i] - input2[i])**2
    return d**(.5)
```

Within the function we first set the value of a new variable d (for distance) to 0. Following this, the function will loop (for i) through each component or "item" of the supplied input objects adding to the variable d the squared differences between the input items. Once the loop is completed and we've reached the end of the supplied input, we return back to the calling function the square root of the summed values stored as d.

When the euclidean_distance function is correctly called with the appropriate parameters, it returns the distance between these parameters in Euclidean space. Euclidean distance is defined as the shortest straight path between two points in a common, uniform geometrical space. As an example, first imagine a simple one-dimensional space, a line, with two points. One point on the line is 8 and the other 64. To calculate the Euclidean distance between these two points, we subtract the second point from the first and square the result and then take the square root. Using the x**y notation in Python to calculate x raised to the power of y, we can find this result with: ((8-64)**2)**.5. Using our euclidean_distance function, we can print these results with:

```
euclidean_distance([8],[64])
```

The basic Python system provides a set of functions embedded within a package called "math" that handles some of these calculations with a little more grace and enables greater readability. Instead of calculating a square root with x**.5 we can ask Python to make the math package available (import math) and use the now available square root or sqrt function. The same goes for calculating squares: we can use pow(x,y) to raise x to y-th power. The revised function now reads as such:

```
import math
def euclidean_distance(input1,input2):
    d = 0
    for i in range(len(input1)):
        d += pow(input1[i] - input2[i]),2)
    return sqrt(d)
```

This trivial example demonstrates that there are many different ways to solve the same problem, some more comprehensible and elegant than others. Elegance in this case includes using the affordances and norms of the programming language – for Python language programs, that means writing code in a manner playfully termed "Pythonic." The choice to use pow and sqrt signals the author's participation in a writing and interpretive community organized around the use of these Pythonic norms.

We can now use our same euclidean_distance function with two-dimensional data. To calculate the shortest distance between two points in a simple x,y coordinate system, we would simply call the function as such: euclidean_distance([-2,2],[2,-1]). The function returns "5.0" as the Euclidean distance between these two points. Higher-dimension data can be supplied in a similar manner. For example, we can take the measurements in centimeters of two Iris flowers that are part of Ronald Fisher's 1936 Iris dataset.[24] For each flower, we have the length and width of the sepal (5.1 and 3.5 for the first flower) and petal (1.4 and 0.2 for the first flower). To calculate the distance between these two flowers in this four-dimensional common, uniform geometrical space, we would simply call our function as such: euclidean_distance([5.1, 3.5, 1.4, 0.2],[4.9, 3.0, 1.4, 0.2])). The "distance" in this shared space between these two flowers is returned as "0.5385164807134502." But what does this distance mean? The possible meanings this distance might have depend on the rest of the dataset. Are these two measurements representative of the phenomena that we wish to

---

24 For an explanation of the dataset, see Ronald A. Fisher, "The Use of Multiple Measurements in Taxonomic Problems," *Annals of Eugenics* 7 (1936): 179–88.

measure (i.e., a natural distribution)? Did we choose the correct parameters (sepal and petal) and measurement metrics (length and width) to make meaningful comparisons?

These simple lines of Python show just some of the possibilities and constraints of programming languages. We have two functions that accomplished the same task but used different methods to reach this result. The revised function is better and yet can be improved in numerous ways. These few lines of code contain within them many assumptions about the input parameters. Taken together, this function encapsulates an understanding of a geometrical space that is in many ways only an ideal.[25] Formally, the function produces the results requested but it operates in concert with its data. This idealized geometric space is created only through data and thus the function cannot be isolated from the "assumptions" held by both the formula it renders as code and its data.[26] This function would typically be used by another that makes use of the returned distances. Euclidean distance, for example, is often used with classification algorithms, including k-nearest neighbor, an algorithm that uses the distances between data labeled as members of existing classes of objects of a similar kind to determine the membership of previously unseen and unlabeled data. The meaning of this code fragment within the implementation of k-nearest neighbor would raise new questions. Is Euclidean distance the appropriate distance metric for this algorithm? What are we attempting to classify? Do these objects all belong to the same space? What might that mean?

Code is created to solve problems. The problem space is cultivated and constrained by understandings of how these problems will present themselves or be presented, especially in the form of data. We can also add the included and instrument-sampled data as another discourse to those mentioned above. Much of these data were ephemeral. They are no longer available, detected and processed in the moment. Some were anticipated and part of the exhaustive testing procedures and others were entirely unpredicted. When examining code, we read and interpret the instructions, imagine or attempt execution. A critical account of the source code of the AGC needs

25 On data vectorization in machine learning as an instance of the problem of constructing abstract spaces, see Adrian Mackenzie, *Machine Learners: Archaeology of a Data Practice* (Cambridge: MIT Press, 2017): 51–74.

26 For more about these assumptions, see James E. Dobson, *Critical Digital Humanities: The Search for a Methodology* (Urbana: University of Illinois Press, 2019), 117–19.

to examine the problem space that gave shape to the code. What were the technical and social constraints? How did these limit the functions and possibilities of the AGC hardware and software? In examining the code, we need to at least attempt to historicize and bring into understanding the execution environment, the computational and cultural situation, that retroactively named this particular text the source code that brought humans to the Moon.

R00002

The AGC and Computing in the 1960s

The digital computer that powered the Apollo 11 Command Module and Lunar Module was sophisticated and equipped with many leading-edge and advanced features despite its compact size and limited fixed and erasable memory capacity.[1] While the majority of computing systems in the 1960s, including the several computers used to compile and debug the AGC software, occupied large spaces in dedicated air-conditioned rooms, the main hardware that made up the AGC computer was stored in a package that measured twenty-four by twelve inches, six inches deep, and weighed a mere seventy pounds.[2] The complete program or software for the AGC was stored in a form of magnetic memory called rope core memory. In this resilient but quite limited storage scheme, a network of wires run through small ferrite core rings store the instructions for the computer. This was fixed, read-only memory as any changes to the instructions required extensive rewiring. The computer was hardwired, as it were, with actual wires that, when selected, signal the 1s and 0s of the binary instructions required to bootstrap or bring the computer into operational status. While the programmers wrote and edited code in their Cambridge, Massachusetts offices, a large group of mostly female workers a few miles away at Raytheon in Waltham — the company that held the NASA contract to produce the computers — programmed and installed the software by twisting and braiding thousands of wires through the ferrite rings.

The transformation of the instructions from symbolic code punched line-by-line through stacks of cards to densely packed sets of wires demonstrates the existence of the multiple shapes and forms — all of which are expressions of the language of computing. Throughout the flow of this language, from initial composition to contemporary methods of digital preservation of the AGC code, we see many such transformations taking place. The code, through many of these conversions, changes its orientation and its form. We might call these code variations versions or perhaps even editions. Calling our attention to the importance of formal features, including style and shape to the interpretation of any digital object, Dennis Tenen would have us recognize these variations as distinct formats of the code.

1   The best guide to the design and operation of the AGC hardware and software is Frank O'Brien, *The Apollo Guidance Computer: Architecture and Operation* (Chichester: Springer, 2010).
2   "Computers in Spaceflight: The NASA Experience," *NASA*, https://history.nasa.gov/computers/Ch2-5.html.

"Formats," Tenen argues, "shape the very structure of interpretation. The seemingly innocuous formatting layer contains the essence of control over the mechanisms of representation. Long a marginal concept in literary theory, formatting is therefore central to the contemporary practice of computational poetics. More than embellishment, formats govern the interface between meaning and matter, thought and page."[3] But it is crucial to recognize that these formats do not necessarily operate in a progressive manner in which the appearance of a new format obsoletes the prior formats. The temporality of code authorship, in particular the code under consideration in this book, is quite complicated; some representations of the AGC code predict future, by which we mean post-processed and collated, forms and formats, while others alter the overall organization of the code and in so doing introduce different meanings to readers and interpreters.

We might understand the multiple formats of the AGC code as a form of what Jay David Bolter and Richard Grusin called remediation.[4] For Bolter and Grusin, remediation is an attribute of media, especially but not limited to digital media, in which the cultural imperatives of immediacy and hypermediacy meet through the multiplication and erasure of media. New media borrow and remake old media in order to produce a sense of immediacy. We can frame newer presentations of the AGC code through the desire to cut out what is now considered extraneous, for example, the line numbers and page headers. In cropping the code and making these headers and numbers marginal, the code becomes more readable, but it has now lost the sense of order that structured the prior format. In producing a remediation of the printed pages in order to present the code as if it were authored in a contemporary high-level programming language, the contemporary programmers have erased the medium-specific features of the earlier code. Of course, the printed pages of code were themselves already making use of a remediated format that erased the medium-specific features of the punch card by turning each card into a line of printed code and by creating page headers and line breaks to increase the readability of the code for the programmers.

We might then apply an additional hermeneutical turn and examine yet another reformatting of the AGC code as it passed through the assembly line

3   Dennis Tenen, *Plain Text: The Poetics of Computation* (Stanford: Stanford University Press, 2017), 130.
4   Jay David Bolter and Richard Grusin, *Remediation: Understanding New Media* (Cambridge: MIT Press, 1999), 4–5, 234–36.

of software production. The instructions on the punched cards were collated and processed by a set of software programs running on a conventional digital computer. The output of the assembler system was the rope wiring diagrams that were sent to Raytheon, the company holding the contract to produce the AGC hardware. The wiring diagrams reformatted the instructions and were installed or programmed through the threading, braiding, and twisting of small, thin wires through sets of rings (**Figure 1**). These memory ropes were used to preserve and package the software for the AGC computer. Each reformatting presents a new material shape for the instructions and incorporates another entire set of labor. That this labor, especially that of the women or "girls" who reformatted the code into twists and braids, was the product of what we might want to call "hidden figures" is a function of both the valuation structures of the 1960s managerial system that unevenly distributed credit and the remediation at the core of all reformatting.[5] These women, like the programmers at the MIT Instrumentation Lab, worked collaboratively, passing the delicate wires back and forth as they embedded instructions into the hardware (**Figure 2**). If we want to study the definitive text that took the astronauts to the Moon, then the proper object of study must include the labor and products of these memory rope programmers. The software development cycle was not limited to the Instrumentation Laboratory and the code was not produced within a closed system of programmers; it required the collaborative work of thousands of people found in numerous organizations and it flowed forward and backward through these networks of people, much like an electrical current through any integrated circuit.

The majority of the code shown throughout this book was authored in one of two fairly low-level single-purpose symbolic languages, Basic (this language has no relation to the much more user-friendly interpreted BA-

---

5   I'm borrowing "hidden figures" in order to gesture toward the presence of many figures, including the African-American human "computers" described by Margot Lee Shetterly's *Hidden Figures: The American Dream and the Untold Story of the Black Women Who Helped Win the Space Race* (New York: William Morrow and Company, 2016). A critical account of women, and especially women of color, as unacknowledged laborers can be found in Lisa Nakamura, "Indigenous Circuits: Navajo Women and the Racialization of Early Electronic Manufacture," *American Quarterly* 66, no. 4 (2014): 919–41. The term "girls" was repeatedly used for the Raytheon workers in a 1965 NASA funded film, *Computer for Apollo,* directed by Russell Morash (Cambridge: MIT Science Reporter, 1965), available at https://www.youtube.com/watch?v=ndvmFlg1WmE.

Figure 1. A Raytheon employee creating Apollo rope memory. Screenshot from *Computer for Apollo*, directed by Russell Morash (Cambridge, MA: MIT Science Reporter, 1965).

Figure 2. Teamwork was required to braid the wires through the cores. Screenshot from *Computer for Apollo*, directed by Russell Morash (Cambridge, MA: MIT Science Reporter, 1965).

SIC, or Beginners All-Purpose Symbolic Instruction Code, language that was developed contemporaneously at Dartmouth College) and what was called Interpretive. The code contains both Basic instructions – the Basic syntax contains only forty instructions or "opcodes," eight of the most common are found in **Table 1** – and the more flexible but much slower Interpretive instructions that were executed by a program called INTERPRETER. Basic was also known as "Yul." It was named Yul by Hugh Blair-Smith because the language was developed for the original AGC Model 1A that was planned to be completed around Christmas time in 1959 (the 1A, according to Blair-Smith, was called the "Christmas Computer"), hence Yul for Yuletide.[6] Yul was not so much a language as a system. It included testing systems and a special piece of software known as an assembler that transformed the Yul code or text, much like other high-level compiled languages like C, into a lower-level machine code and finally produced the wiring diagrams mentioned above.

The Yul system was designed to enable the programmers to quickly compose, edit, and test code before it was generated as the read-only, permanent instructions stored in the AGC's rope memory. Like several other programming languages of the period, the two languages used in this code are fixed format languages. This means that the format of the code was imagined and printed on pages needed to take a specific form in order for conversion routines to produce the correct instructions for the digital computer that would eventually execute the instructions. The AGC code was written and edited under numerous constraints, including the rigidly fixed format required by the punch card and its associated hardware as well as the limited syntax of its major programming languages.

The AGC software was designed in an era before software as we understand it today was invented. The systems and code were imagined, designed, and edited not in a digital environment, with the array of graphical display devices, easily movable sections of text, searching mechanisms, and versioning information, but almost entirely in print and on paper. This high-tech digital computer system belonged to the world of print and it was thus imagined by the software engineers as an almost literary object.

6   Hugh Blair-Smith, "Annotations to Eldon Hall's Journey to the Moon," *Apollo Guidance Computer History Project*, February 1997, https://authors.library.caltech.edu/5456/1/hrst.mit.edu/hrs/apollo/public/blairsmith.htm.

TC	Transfer Control
CCS	Count, Compare, Skip
INDEX	Modify Next Instruction
XCH	Exchange
CS	Clear and Subtract
TS	Transfer to Storage
AD	Add and Count on Overflow
MP	Multiply

Table 1. Major Basic or Yul Instructions

The literary "print" metaphor drives the majority of our thinking about the prospects for interpreting the code. For while it was the depositing of the digitized code within Github, a collaborative online code repository, that initially brought the text of the Apollo Guidance Computer code to our attention, the metaphor of the printed code as an imagined and interpretable text remains our doorway into this project and into its historical moment. The programmers had to work simultaneously with at least two different formats of printed code: collated code listings and punch cards. In his memoir, *Sunburst and Luminary: An Apollo Memoir* (2018), Apollo Guidance Computer programmer Don Eyles links the writing of code to the writing of prose by reflecting on writing as a process: "Some of us wrote out our programs fully on paper forms before we sat down. Others programmed as they punched. I usually started with rough notes and wrote very much as I am writing at this moment."[7]

The AGC code is a highly revised, co-authored text. It was written line by line. Each line of eighty-character instructions was entered by hand, punched on an IBM 026 keypunch. But the code was imagined, always, and edited as a listing — it was collated and printed in page form, after being run through (each reading of the code was called a "pass" and several "passes" were required to fully format and process the list of instructions) different assembler programs. These assembler programs ran on the same larger general-purpose computer that processed the stack of punch cards. During the time of the Apollo 11 mission, this computer was a Honeywell 800. The final pass was known as the "wiring diagrammer" and it produced the wiring diagram tapes that were sent directly to Raytheon.[8] The AGC code was thus produced under numerous constraints, including the rigidly fixed format required by the IBM 026 keypunch mechanism along with the Honeywell 800 card reader and the limited syntax of its major programming languages. The programmers, therefore, had to be flexible in their imagination of what the code would look like and how it would function when it was transformed into these other formats.

Consider the now iconic image of Margaret Hamilton with the stack of AGC code almost reaching her own height (**Figure 3**). This image referenc-

7   Don Eyles, *Sunburst and Luminary: An Apollo Memoir* (Boston: Four Point Press, 2018), 56.
8   Ramon Alonso, J. Halcombe Laning, Jr., and Hugh Blair-Smith, *E-1077: Preliminary MOD 3C Programmers Manual* (Cambridge: MIT Instrumentation Laboratory, 1961), 50.

Figure 3. Margaret Hamilton standing next to stack of Apollo Guidance Computer code. Courtesy of the MIT Museum.

es and reworks other depictions of programmers, especially women, with the material embodiment of code. Computer company advertising, for many years of its early existence, used images of women appearing next to stacks of punch cards, storage devices, and other equipment. This photograph of Hamilton references and reconfigures the advertising image to position her and her body as the signature that authorizes the presented code. The code is "embodied" both in the sense of the presentation of the complete body of the text, as well as the reference image, the human body, that serves to measure the length of the code. The concept of software and the engineering of software were essentially being invented at this moment. Comparing the code to the body made it concrete by presenting it in a familiar form and scene.

That code that we see represented as stacks of printed pages or displayed as modular functions and routines stored in separate files within the Github repository was initially authored in short eighty-column segments on 3¼ x 7½ IBM paper punch-cards (referred to simply as "cards" with the body of the code). A card reader sorted and compiled the individual cards into the text of the complete code for the AGC and it was then printed on wide pages on a Honeywell printer. The code authors produced small sets of instructions and commentary on the code on individual punch cards, but imagined the collaboratively constructed code as a numerically ordered set of cards, with each card forming a line of code and eventually printed on pages. The code presents and understands itself in paginated terms. There are numerous times in which the code references other "paragraphs" and pages of the code – there were 1,743 pages of code in the "LUMINARY 1A" portion of the AGC code of July 14, 1969. In the imaged scans of the printed code that are available, we can see that the text of the code was printed on a continuous stream of paper with alternating colored lines. Each printed page (see **Figure 4**) contained a short header that provided metadata about the assembly and printing of the code, including the revision, the current date and time, and the page number.

The code and language used throughout the AGC project is simple and rather utilitarian. As mentioned above, this was due to the limited memory of the AGC computer and the constraints of the coding environment. The following table reproduces information from the Programmer's Manual and

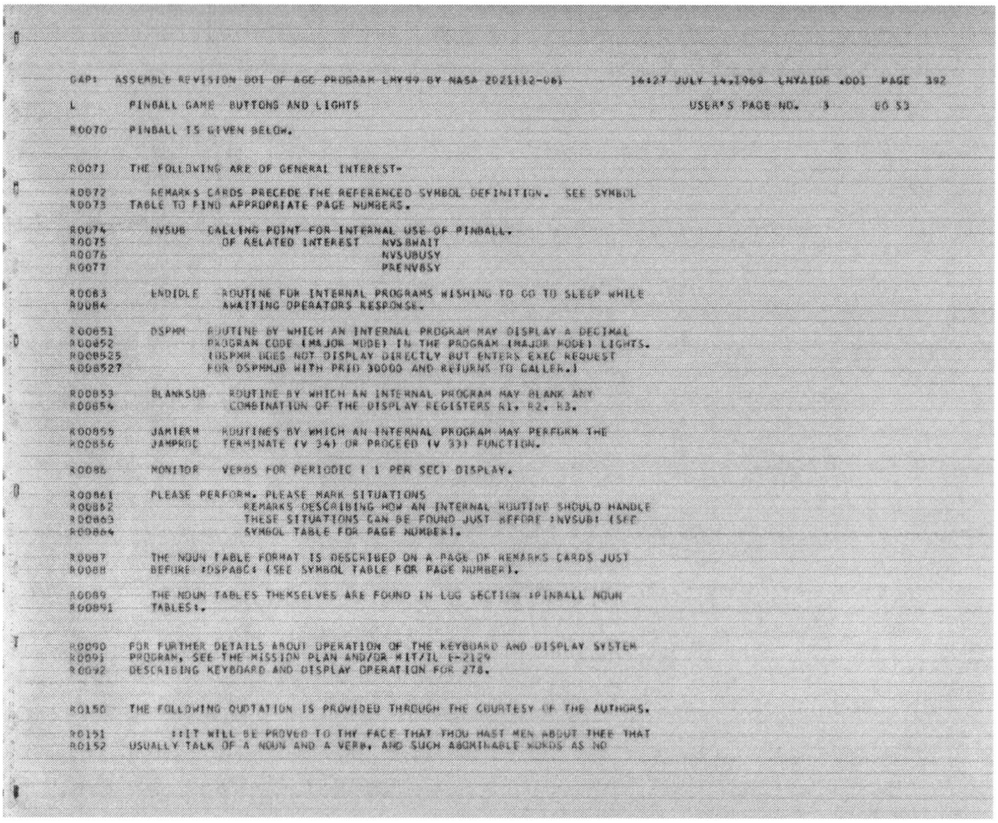

```
GAP: ASSEMBLE REVISION 001 OF AGC PROGRAM LMY99 BY NASA 2021112-061          16:27 JULY 14,1969 LMYAIDE .001 PAGE 392

L       PINBALL GAME  BUTTONS AND LIGHTS                              USER'S PAGE NO.  3       60 53

R0070   PINBALL IS GIVEN BELOW.

R0071   THE FOLLOWING ARE OF GENERAL INTEREST-

R0072      REMARKS CARDS PRECEDE THE REFERENCED SYMBOL DEFINITION.  SEE SYMBOL
R0073   TABLE TO FIND APPROPRIATE PAGE NUMBERS.

R0074      NVSUB   CALLING POINT FOR INTERNAL USE OF PINBALL.
R0075                OF RELATED INTEREST   NVSBWAIT
R0076                                      NVSUBUSY
R0077                                      PRENVBSY

R0083      ENDIDLE   ROUTINE FOR INTERNAL PROGRAMS WISHING TO GO TO SLEEP WHILE
R0084                AWAITING OPERATORS RESPONSE.

R00851     DSPMM   ROUTINE BY WHICH AN INTERNAL PROGRAM MAY DISPLAY A DECIMAL
R00852             PROGRAM CODE (MAJOR MODE) IN THE PROGRAM (MAJOR MODE) LIGHTS.
R008525            (DSPMM DOES NOT DISPLAY DIRECTLY BUT ENTERS EXEC REQUEST
R008527            FOR DSPMMJB WITH PRIO 30000 AND RETURNS TO CALLER.)

R00853     BLANKSUB   ROUTINE BY WHICH AN INTERNAL PROGRAM MAY BLANK ANY
R00854                COMBINATION OF THE DISPLAY REGISTERS R1, R2, R3.

R00855     JAMTERM   ROUTINES BY WHICH AN INTERNAL PROGRAM MAY PERFORM THE
R00856     JAMPROC   TERMINATE (V 34) OR PROCEED (V 33) FUNCTION.

R0086      MONITOR   VERBS FOR PERIODIC ( 1 PER SEC) DISPLAY.

R00861     PLEASE PERFORM, PLEASE MARK SITUATIONS
R00862                REMARKS DESCRIBING HOW AN INTERNAL ROUTINE SHOULD HANDLE
R00863                THESE SITUATIONS CAN BE FOUND JUST BEFORE :NVSUB: (SEE
R00864                SYMBOL TABLE FOR PAGE NUMBER).

R0087      THE NOUN TABLE FORMAT IS DESCRIBED ON A PAGE OF REMARKS CARDS JUST
R0088      BEFORE :DSPABC: (SEE SYMBOL TABLE FOR PAGE NUMBER).

R0089      THE NOUN TABLES THEMSELVES ARE FOUND IN LOG SECTION :PINBALL NOUN
R00891     TABLES:.

R0090   FOR FURTHER DETAILS ABOUT OPERATION OF THE KEYBOARD AND DISPLAY SYSTEM
R0091   PROGRAM, SEE THE MISSION PLAN AND/OR MIT/IL E-2129
R0092   DESCRIBING KEYBOARD AND DISPLAY OPERATION FOR 278.

R0150   THE FOLLOWING QUOTATION IS PROVIDED THROUGH THE COURTESY OF THE AUTHORS.

R0151         ::IT WILL BE PROVED TO THY FACE THAT THOU HAST MEN ABOUT THEE THAT
R0152   USUALLY TALK OF A NOUN AND A VERB, AND SUCH ABOMINABLE WORDS AS NO
```

Figure 4. AGC Source Code, page 392.

illustrates the prescribed content for each column or punch card position for each line of the AGC code.[9]

Columns	1–7	Card Number and Card Content Control
Columns	8	Vertical Spacing Control
Columns	9–16	Location Field
Columns	18–23	Operation Field
Columns	25–40	Address Field
Columns	41–80	Remarks Field

Table 2.1: Punch card organization

The card numbers, columns 2–7, indicated what would become the line number of the card when it was collated and printed. Like the line numbers used in the popular BASIC programming language, these card and line numbers were used to organize code and to enable some basic editing and revision. These were incrementing numbers and each card inserted into the card reader was required to be a larger number than the previous card. It appears that the programmers planned to use four- or five-digit numbers (the majority are five digit numbers). If blank, the value of empty columns was equivalent to zero, enabling the proper sorting of any number of cards. The first card of the Luminary 1A program was numbered R00001 and was followed by R00002 and then R000025. The addition of the sixth column for the third card demonstrates an important feature of the code: it was designed to enable the addition of new code and the minor revision of existing code without renumbering and thus repunching the entire body of the code. This is enabled projective thinking — the imagination of future revisions by leaving possible empty space, an area of expansion and breathing room for the existing code. If new code was required to add a feature or extend particular instructions, these additional cards using six-column numbers

9   Ibid., 54.

could be inserted between existing cards that used five-column numbers. With this scheme, nine lines could be added (XXXXX1–XXXXX9) without introducing a major revision. To correct a minor error, the programmer would just need to revise that single card.

The cards beginning with the character R were known as "remarks cards." While the Yul language specifications defines specific column markers, for free-form explanatory or other forms of commentary in each card, these remarks cards mark the entire card space as remarks. These cards, like the contents of columns 41–80, lack any explicit requirements or standards. Remarks cards, such as the first three cards invoked above, were used for various functions. At the most simple level, most code is marked by two voices: the code and embedded remarks or commentary. Commentary is a supplement; not necessary for execution but essential for its comprehension and future modification.[10] Code commentary speaks to the past, this is how this works and why we did this, but primarily it addresses future readers – reminders, warnings, justifications. The cards that make up the page of code in **Figure 4** provide explanatory notes about the code that appears in the following cards. Cards R0072 and R0073 explain the general purpose of the remarks cards throughout the code: REMARKS CARDS PRECEDE THE REFERENCED SYMBOL DEFINITION. SEE SYMBOL TABLE TO FIND APPROPRIATE PAGE NUMBERS. With these statements the programmers make reference to two of the major forms of the code: the cards that make up the individual lines and the transformed and paginated text printed on 11 × 15-inch paper. These remarks address future readers of the code and provide them with an introduction or preface to the text that will follow. Remarks cards and the remarks columns of the cards are outside of the code – they are assembled and printed but never executed, never transformed into wiring diagrams – but still contained within the text of the code. The reference or pointer to a specialized index or table of contents points to the way in which the programmers understand their code to be a printed text. The addition of new cards, even those making use of six-column card numbers, would alter page numbers, thus there are references to abstract pages rather than specific page numbers.

10 On code commentary, see Amy Hunt, "Not Your Typical Prose: Documenting Software,"
    MALS thesis, Dartmouth College, 2016 and Stuart Mawler, "Executable Texts: Programs as
    Communications Devices and Their Use in Shaping High-tech Culture," MSc thesis, Virginia Polytechnic Institute and State University, 2007.

If we are to understand references to the appearance of the code as abstract, we should read the signs of authorship as even more obscure. Determining the authorship of any collaboratively edited text is difficult. Because of the sparseness of the syntax and diction available and the heavily edited and revised nature of large projects such as the AGC, code remains especially impenetrable to determining authorship. The authorship of code might best be theorized in terms of a function or collaborative group. The code was written and edited collaboratively, but that did not lend much coherence to the organization and form of the code. Fred Martin explains: "[We] had no standards. We had no programming standards. Each group or each little entity would have a style. I think when we got into project management, I did try, to some extent, to get some standardization. But it was hard. I think people used different expressions for constants in their programs."[11] At several locations within the code there are self-referential comments referring to "the authors" as originators for the commentary and code. I will thus follow their lead and unless there are specific markers, we refer to the AGC code as authored by "the programmers" throughout our interpretation and analysis.

The following code segment tells us that Margaret Hamilton is the author of this particular program, which itself appears to be four different programs:

```
# PROGRAM NAME: PREREAD, READACCS, SERVICER, AVERAGE G.
# MOD NO. 00 BY M. HAMILTON     DEC. 12, 1966
#
# FUNCTIONAL DESCRIPTION
```

The code displayed here in these lines has been transformed from the paginated number lines into a format that corresponds to contemporary coding practices. These are lines of code as they appear in the Github repository for the Apollo 11 AGC code. Instead of numbered remarks cards, commentary appears in lines or sections of lines beginning with the # character. This conforms to coding norms in a number of more contemporary programming

---

11 "Different Programming Styles," *Apollo Guidance Computer History Project: Second Conference*, September 14, 2001, https://authors.library.caltech.edu/5456/1/hrst.mit.edu/hrs/apollo/public/conference2/styles.htm.

languages. The text or other characters following the # are not interpreted. Each of the above lines would have been a separate remarks card. The first line glosses the purpose of this particular section or program within the body of the AGC code. We know that this is the first version or modification of the code, but the numbering scheme here includes double-digit zeros, a variation of the modification scheme used in other sections and subroutines.

The following lines provide another example of what was a set of remarks cards, a set of cards introducing code with a more complex revision history:

```
# SUBROUTINE NAME:  TFFCONIC              DATE:  01.29.67
# MOD NO: 0                               LOG SECTION:  TIME OF FREE FALL
# MOD BY: RR BAIRNSFATHER
# MOD NO: 1 MOD BY: RR BAIRNSFATHER DATE: 11 APR 67
# MOD NO: 2 MOD BY: RR BAIRNSFATHER DATE: 21 NOV 67 ADD MOON MU.
# MOD NO: 3 MOD BY: RR BAIRNSFATHER DATE: 21 MAR 68 ACCEPT DIFFERENT EARTH/
MOON SCALES
```

In the above, we see several modifications or revisions of the code. Each of these "mods" is numbered in sequential order, beginning with 0 for the first modification (unlike the double-digit mod in the previous example) and incremented by one for each major revision. What constitutes enough change to introduce a new "mod" is not exactly clear from the code or the manuals. How much of the code should change for the mod counter to be incremented? Any modification of the code at all? Major changes?

What we would now call the programming environment for writing and editing code was entirely paper-based. Because of the nature of the input devices, the punch card system, and the use of other programs to pass through and assemble the code, it needed to undergo numerous runs through a transformation that moved and organized stacks of individual cards into paginated, ordered form. The printed pages that provide the historical record of the AGC code demonstrate the extent to which the programmers needed to keep these different forms active in their imagination of the code at all times. The AGC code provides a palimpsestic record of this process; it bears the traces of its composition and revision. These lines of code offer up a snapshot, a frozen image of a collaboratively edited and dynamically changing text.

Tracing Memory and Executing Code

The Apollo Guidance Computer code is complex and frequently difficult to understand. It is hard to follow for several reasons. The limited number of instructions and the lack of abstracted or higher-level libraries providing commonly used subroutines means that the code needed to be as compact and minimal as possible. When reading the code, we need to trace the "line" of execution and follow instructions and data through numerous obscure and abstruse subroutines. In following these instructions, we need to keep in mind the current state of the computer and memory and in particular the present state of a special location or register known as the accumulator. The accumulator was used by the programmers to store the current value of the last arithmetic or logical operation.

The small sections of code shown in this section were compiled, executed, and inspected using two tools from the open-source Virtual AGC environment: yaYUL, the code compiler that generates "core-rope" objects and yaAGC, the AGC emulator and debugger that executes compiled core-ropes.[12] The following lines of a fragment of a Basic program for the AGC demonstrates how one would write a program to add together two simple decimal numbers and save the result to a section of erasable memory:

```
        BLOCK   2
SUM     EQUALS  10
A       EQUALS  0

        CA   VALUE1
        AD   VALUE2
        TS   SUM
        TC   EXIT

VALUE1     DEC  5
VALUE2     DEC  7
```

12 These tools are provided as part of the fantastic resource that is the open-source VirtualAGC environment. The code for these two tools (they were written in C and can be compiled on several different platforms) can be found with the rest of the environment at: https://github.com/virtualagc/.

```
EXIT
```

The first line contains an instruction to tell the computer where to store the code, which block of memory to use. The next two lines assign names to specific memory locations. The name A is shorthand for the accumulator. The memory location name SUM is used, in this code fragment, as the storage location using a 10-bit memory address, to which we will transfer the output from the accumulator. The two numbers to be added are stored as variables. These variables, VALUE1 and VALUE2, are defined as a particular type of number, decimals. The DEC instruction tells the compiler that the variable name appearing to the left will contain a decimal and assigns to this variable the value on the right. Decimals, with either single, double, or triple precision, are one datatype used by the Basic/Yul programming language, and others include tables and vectors. Within the debugger provided by the AGC emulator, we can access a list of these variables with the "info variables" command:

```
File sum.agc:
var VALUE1;
var VALUE2;
```

To display the stored or current values of these variables, we can use the print command:

```
print/d VALUE1
$1 = +5
```

The +5 indicates that VALUE1 was stored as a decimal value with a positive value. To add these two variables, we first "Clear and Add" (CA) the value of VALUE1 to the accumulator. Executing this code instruction by instruction, we watch the value of the accumulator change:

```
print/d A
$1 = +0
next
print/d A
$1 = +5
```

Once the accumulator contains the value of VALUE1, we can Add (AD) the value of VALUE2 to the accumulator:

```
next
print/d A
$1 = +12
```

With the value we want available in the accumulator register, we can Transfer to Storage (TS) this value to the storage location SUM and then Transfer Control (TC) to a subroutine named EXIT that performs no function:

```
TS SUM
TC EXIT
```

We can print the contents of the memory location referenced as SUM and find the correct result:

```
print/d SUM
$1 = +12
```

Building on the above set of instructions, we can see how we might begin to implement the Euclidean distance metric mentioned in the previous chapter using a simple set of Basic primitives. In the extended list, the language provides an instruction to calculate the square of a number store in the accumulator called SQUARE. Using a temporary storage location, we can subtract two numbers and then square the result. This code fragment adds the instruction to Subtract (SU), Square (SQUARE), and exchanges the output of the L register used to store the result by the SQUARE instruction with another erasable memory location (OUTPUT):

```
        BLOCK    2
OUTP    EQUALS   10
A       EQUALS   0
TEMP    EQUALS   11
        CA   VALUE2
        TS   TEMP
        CA   VALUE1
        EXTEND
        SU   TEMP
        EXTEND
        SQUARE
        LXCH OUTP
        TC   EXIT
VALUE1      DEC  8
VALUE2      DEC  64
EXIT
```

Moonbit:
Erasure Poems
Derived from Apollo 11 Source Code

Part One:
Comanche

Comanche

Part of the source code
for Colossus 2A, AKA Comanche 055
for the Command Module's (CM)
Apollo Guidance Computer (AGC), for Apollo 11

Comanche by NASA
entry initialization routine
state +6 startent
come here #goneby #gonepast

may be noise
return via ref coords
since 1st guessbad
clear clear lunaflag

sequencing is as follows:
huntest the super-circular phase
spacecraft in pitch and yaw
an exit is made

start targeting
come here
go get it
getvel getunitv geteta getangle dad

dad argument is zero
sign may become erratic very near target due to loss of precision

Pinball Noun Tables

Straight fractional arithmetic
whole hours whole minutes seconds

(ALARM) (STRAIGHT) (ALARM)
interpretation use arithmetic

nautical miles   use constant code numbers
velocity   use noun tables

elevation degrees   use octal loads
inertia   use major part

thrust moment   use minor part
position 6   use decimal only

drag acceleration   use display verb
alarm if an attempt is made to load

reading routines
if the noun is mixed or normal

if the noun is mixed
astronaut total attitude

first mixed noun
please perform

time of landing
time to perigee
time of ignition
time of event
time to go

Of Next Burn

Target   Each
Azimuth   Whole

Apogee   Latitude
Longitude   Attitude

this vehicle weight   other vehicle weight

splash error   heads up

range to splash   star code

horizon data   half unit sun or planet

preferred attitude   each whole yoptics

Alarm and Abort

Alarm
Alarm 2
Bortent
Larment

Add super bits

is anything in failreg
yes try next reg

returns to the user
from the astronaut

leave L alone
don't move

whimper
resume
enema

Don't do poodoo. Do bailout.

mr. klean
curtains inhint

save users
don't move

To Load into Smode

Starting verb erasable
memory fixed memory

octal everything
normal and alarm
in idle loop

the failreg set
turns on the alarm light
the operator
initiated fresh start

three failregs
since the last man
show-banksum
the bugger word
erasable accomplished

exception is a restart
unless there is evidence to doubt
in which case program
equals   selfret
equals   is it necessary
equals   new job

illegal option
go to idle loop

Charley, come in here

Waitlist

Call a program
(Called a task)
which is to begin
the meaning of these lists

follow   warnings   taskover
under interrupt inhibited
time in centiseconds
to task start

twiddle is for eliminating the need
saving a word
twiddle is like waitlist
fresh start   endtask   all counters ticking

processing time and the possibility
if twiddling task will remain in L
fixdelay and vardelay
saved during delay

distinguishable by its
drift flag   someone else   compensate for coefficients
enable every delay
overflow has occurred

thus there need be no concern over a previous or imminent overflow
dummy task   fixed it   no room in the inn
can't get here   only the first exit to the caller of longcall
now exit properly

Goneby

Gone past target
neg if will fall short

this way for dap
count tinythet enter

scale up factor up storekat
forehunt #initialize huntest

must go after forehunt for restarts
otherwise lewd barely1 fact2

truncated halve push overlapping
final phase range

DAD DAD
DAD DAD

Getlewd storedlewd #if lewd+dlewd neg
Roll over top, regardless

push up lad ballistic phase
push up here

prefinal came but of
steeroff #precautionary

back table jj cannot be zero
extend extend interpret

and fall into glimiter section
dance   disk and dance

Fresh Start

Slap1
Man initiated fresh start
execute startsub

clear fail registers
initialize flagwords
goprog major code change enema

Mr. Klean comes here from pinball
does most of the work
same story

POOKLEAN GOJAM
we are in a restart loop
MASK EXTEND START

(This might happen again)
Enema killed waitlist
and biases thus

Do not use enema without consulting POOH people
Depressed rand reject
standby

GOTOPOOH rendezvous
to continue
from astronaut

Star Tables

```
Startab              X
COUNT stars          Y
# star 37            Z

# star 36            X
# star 35            Y
# star 34            Z

# star 33            X
# star 32            Y
# star 31            Z

# star 30            X
# star 29            Y
# star 28            Z

# star 27            X
# star 26            Y
# star 25            Z

# star 24            X
# star 23            Y
# star 22            Z

# star 21            X
# star 20            Y
# star 19            Z

# star 18            X
# star 17            Y
# star 16            Z
```

```
# star 15          X
# star 14          Y
# star 13          Z

# star 12          X
# star 11          Y
# star 10          Z

# star 9           X
# star 8           Y
# star 7           Z

# star 6           X
# star 5           Y
# star 4           Z

# star 3           X
# star 2           Y
# star 1           Z
```

Time of Free Fall

Add moon
Accept different earth/moon scales

angular momentum
mu semi latus rectum

it is the user who knows
if earth origin

if moon origin
the user must release

at present it is not deemed necessary
the program will save earth or moon

call yourmu
debris from dad

save keep get store push
not so accurate, but ok

bairnsfather accept different moon
improve a general conic

not meaningful
not defined

correct
alarms: none

near Earth add accept
the free-fall call call arbitrary

user must positive flight time
this option is no longer used

and will be destroyed
not touched

left by user
continue free fall

otherwise save

Jet Selection Logic

```
#       BIT NO. 11  10  9       NO. OF ROLL JETS
#
#          0   0   0              -2
#          0   0   1              -1
#          0   1   0               0
#          0   1   1              +1
#          1   0   0              +2
```

Examine the translation
pick up for lem

no lem zero all requests
pitch flag for real quad failures

if failures are present
look up

yaw jet commands
rbdfail masks for pitch perform

roll commands
contain the magnitude

an undesireable roll
no failures may be satisfied simultaneously

in which case the astronaut should
satisfy the roll commands

facilitate the logic
translations can produce rotations

nevertheless, we must
it is necessary

Lunar and Solar Ephemerides Subroutines

The sun and the moon relative to the Earth
by the user

in the computer
in the form of

a 15 day interval
the position vectors of the sun and the moon

velocity vector of the moon
of the sun calling time

at the center of the range
erasable data

of the sun
in meters res

Erasable Assignments

X equals start
registers included
the nature of permanence
the mission
for one purpose
and cannot be shared
it need not be
active in parallel
probably temporary
out means output
thrust equals 55
rolljets equals 6
flagwords freeflag goneby glokfail
kflag lunaflag quitflag
knownflg rndvzflg
sourceflg stateflg
strikflag targ1flg targ2flg
of state without
solar perturbations
moon is sphere of earth
is sphere of influence
Moonbit primary planet
different same
running not running
initiated not initiated
in time critical
not in time critical
allowed not allowed
two jet rcs burn
four jet rcs burn
compute earth
use fixed moon
sighting landmark
sighting star
disregard radar
steering burn

Erasable Assignments 2.0

First pass succeeding
pass thru star
occulted star not occulted

matrix valid for W
matrix invalid for
no higher priority

transearth slow down is not slow
is desired
body rates computed

do not terminate
tig has arrived
astronaut has astronaut has not

on lunar surface surfbit   closure exists
infinity required
inhibited near 360 degrees

moon vicinity earth vicinity
are not equals due to wiring
state erase

interpretive trace
mixnoun fetch
code equals must mixtemp

switch bit within the switch word
erase dynamically
erase location associated with job

blankset erase
pushloc erase
priority erase

erase present job and work area
erase space craft
erase staralign

Do not share.
If other users materialize
holdflag

low thrust
longexit erase
restart star

save wango
rollfire slope
rollword last variable

equals zeroed
is zeroed Saturn boost
argument for Polly

body3 body2 body1
oldboy1 oldboy2 oldboy3
return-to-earth

Antenna

Salt gets
us here
on and
aligned
interpret
earth=0
moon=2
move ratt
to prevent
wipeout
stable
member
zero out
yawang
transformation
call store R
NoAdjust
Revolutions Scaled
Is Bit 5 still on
MASK BIT5
EXTEND
ENDEXT

No, we have been answered

Part Two:
64 Found Bits (8 poems made of 8 octets of erasure)

ANGLFIND

\# Page 399 **PICK UP** CURRENT CDU ANGLES
\# STORE THE INITIAL S/C **ANGLES**
\# **COMPUTE** THE TRANSFORMATION FROM $2
                    MIS   TRANSPOSE
\# **COMPUTE** THE TRANSFORMATION **FROM**
FINAL TO STABLE
\# TMIS = **TRANSPOSE**(MIS) SCALED BY 2
PROCEED ACCORDING TO ITS MAGNITUDE

\# **CALCULATE** AM

	DLOAD	**DAD**	
		CHECKMAX	
	EXIT		\# MANEUVER LESS THAN 0.25 DEG
	IN**HINT**		\# GO **DIRECTL**Y INTO ATTITUDE HOLD
	CS	ONE	\# ABOUT COMMANDED ANGLES
	TS	HOLDFLAG	\# **NOGO WILL STOP** ANY RATE AND SET UP
	TC	LOADC**DUD**	\# **GOOD RETURN**
	TCF	NO**GO**	
CHECK**MAX**	D**LOAD**	DSU	
		AM	
		MAXANG	
	BPL	**VLOAD**	
		ALTCALC	\# **UNIT**
		COF**SKEW**	\# COFSKEW
		STORECOF	\# COF **IS THE MANEUVER** AXIS

SEE **IF** MANEUVER GOES THRU
I AM GREATER THAN

                                                          SCALED B 4

CALCULATE ROOT   **$ ROOT 2**
$ROOT2

                                               $ROOT

DETERMINE **LARGE**ST
ADJUST ACCORDINGLY

METHOD1   **LOCSKIRT**
METHOD2

          OCSKIRT

                    SIGN OF UZ OPPOSITE
     GOTO   **CSKIRT**
METHOD3   **MATRIX OPERATIONS MULTIPLIES** 2 3X3 MATRICES
          AND LEAVES
          DEFINE SKIRT

          PUSH
               GOTO
MATRIX

                         # **ENTER** WITH MATRIX IN PD LIST
RETURN WITH
MINANG   DEC   .00069375
MAXANG   DEC   .472222
LOCK CONSTANTS

NGL = BUFFER ANGLE (TO **AVOID DIVISIONS BY ZERO**) = 2 DEGREES
SD   DEC .433015   # = **SIN**(D)   **$2**
K3S1   DEC .86603   # = **SIN**(D)   **$2**
K4   DEC -.25   # = **-COS**(D)   **$2**
K4SQ   DEC .125   # = **COS**(D)COS(D)   **$2**
SNGLCD   DEC .008725   # = **SIN(NGL)COS(D)** $2
CNGL   DEC .499695   # = COS(NGL)   **$2**
READCDUK   IN**HINT**   # LOAD T(MPAC) **WITH THE CURRENT** CDU ANGLES

TO COMPUTE DIRECTION SET STORE   LOOPS LOAD   **LOGIC THE SIN**
WITH THE SIN **SCALED STA R**   PUSH PUSH UP   EQUALS
WHERE U IS A UNIT A IS THE ANGLE
CONTAINS THE TERMS   PUSH   **DAD**
CAN BE WRITTEN AS*** THE **COMPLEMENT**
WILL BE LEFT   WHERE
QUADRANT   **TERMINATING**
ZEROERROR   **# GOODEND**   ENDOFJOB

CM_BODY_ATTITUDE

```
BODY ANGLES VALID AT PIP TIME
SAVED DURING      READ
LET INTERPRETER SET      POSE
INTPRET               # COME HERE      VIA    AVE    EXIT
PROVIDE A STABLE
UN FOR THE END
OF THE TERMINAL PHASE.
SPVQUIT               DEC .019405                  # 1000/ 2 VS

          TIX,1  VLOAD              # IF V-VQUIT POS, BRANCH
                 CM/POSE2           # SAME UYA IN OLDUYA
                 OLDUYA               # OTHERWISE CONTINUE TO USE OLDUYA
CM/POSE2  STORE  UYA/2          #                    REF COORDS
STORE     OLDUYA               # RESTORE, OR SAVE AS CASE MAY BE.
          VXV    VCOMP
                 UXA/2          # FINISH OBTAINING TRAJECTORY TRIAD.
                               # NOISE WON'T OVFL


          TLOAD     EXIT     # ANGLES IN MPAC IN THE ORDER
                             # -( (ROLL, BETA, ALFA) /180)/2
                 6D          # THESE VALUES CORRECT AT PIPUP TIME.
# BASIC SUBROUTINE TO UPDATE ATTITUDE ANGLES
     INHINT
                      # MUST REMAIN INHINTED UNTIL UPDATE OF BODY
                      # ANGLES, SO THAT GAMDIFSW IS VALID FIRST PASS
                      # INDICATOR.

          MASK   BIT11     # GAMDIFSW=94D BIT11    INITLY=0
          EXTEND           # DON'T CALC GAMA DOT UNTIL HAVE FORMD
                           # ONE DIFFERENCE.
          BZF    DOGAMDOT  # IS OK, GO ON.
          ADS    CM/FLAGS  # KNOW BIT IS 0
          TC     NOGAMDOT  # SET GAMDOT = 0
DOGAMDOT  CS     L
          AD     GAMA      # DEL GAMA/360= T GAMDOT/360
```

```
NOGAMDOT   CA     ZERO              # COME HERE INHINTED
           TS     EBANK
                  EBANK=            PHSNAME5
                  EXTEND
           DCA    REPOSADR          # THIS ASSUMES THAT THE TC  PHASCHNG
           DXCH   PHSNAME5          # IS NOT CHANGED IN         OCT 10035
           CA     EBAOG
           TS     EBANK


           EXTEND                     # IGNORE GAMDOT IF LEQ .5 DEG/SEC
           BZMF   +3                # SET GAMDOT=+0 AS TAG IF TOO SMALL
NOGAMDOT   CA     ZERO              # COME HERE INHINTED
           TC     CORANGOV          # CORRECT FOR OVFL IF ANY
           SU     ROLL/PIP          # GET INCR SINCE PIPUP
           AD     ROLL/180          # ONLY SINGLE OVFL POSSIBLE.
           CS     MPAC +2            # GET (ALFA EUL/180) /2
           DOUBLE                    # SAME AS FOR ROLL.  NEEDED FOR EXT


REDOPOSE   EXTEND                    # RE-STARTS COME HERE
           DCA    TEMPROLL
           DXCH   ROLL/180
           TC     INTPRET           # CAN'T TC DANZIG AFTER PHASCHNG.
CM/POSE3   VLOAD    ABVAL           # RETURN FROM CM/ATUP.
                  VN          # 2(-7) M/CS
           STORE    VMAGI              # FOR DISPLAY ON CALL.
           GOTOPOSEXIT               # ENDEXIT, STARTENT, OR SCALEPOP.


           INDEX  A
           CA     LIMITS
           ADS    L
           TC     Q             # COSTS 2 MCT TO USE.  SEE ANGOVCOR.
-KVSCALE   2DEC   -.81491944    # -12800/(2 VS .3048)
TCDU       DEC    .1            # TCDU = .1 SEC.
           EBANK=   AOG
REPOSADR   2CADR    REDOPOSE
```

SOLVE VARIOUS PROBLEMS INVOLVING THE TRAJECTORY PRODUCED BY A
CENTRAL INVERSE-SQUARE FORCE ACTING ON A POINT MASS
A GENERAL USAGE POINT-OF-VIEW WAS TAKEN IN FORMULATING,
THAT ONLY ONE SET OF CODING IS USED, WHETHER THE
EARTH, MOON, OR ANY OTHER CELESTIAL BODY IS SPECIFIED AS THE CENTRAL
TO INTERRUPT EACH OTHER. IT IS UP TO THE USER TO GUARANTEE THIS
MOD BY KRAUSE   ASSEMBLY -- COLOSSUS 103 AND SUNDANCE 222
MOD NO. -- 2 (AUGUST 1968)

THIS SUBROUTINE, GIVEN AN INITIAL STATE VECTOR AND THE DESIRED
BE UPDATED ALONG A CONIC TRAJECTORY, COMPUTES THE NEW,
UPDATED STATE VECTOR. THE TRAJECTORY MAY BE ANY CONIC
SECTION -- CIRCULAR, ELLIPTIC, PARABOLIC, HYPERBOLIC, OR
RECTILINEAR WITH RESPECT TO THE EARTH OR THE MOON. THE
                        DLOAD   DAD
TDESIRED
SOMETIME

DEBRIS --PARAMETERS WHICH MAY BE OF USE --
RTNLAMB (SP), PLUS PUSHLIST REGISTER 0 THROUGH 41D
ADDITIONAL INTERPRETIVE SWITCHES USED -- INFINFLG, 360SW,
SLOPESW, ORDERSW
FUNCTIONAL DESCRIPTION --
TRUE-ANOMALY-DIFFERENCE THROUGH WHICH THE
CIRCLE, ELLIPSE, PARABOLA, OR HYPERBOLA WITH RESPECT TO THE
EARTH OR THE MOON. THE USE OF THE SUBROUTINE CAN BE

FIRSTIME
          SR1   BOFF
                   DELDEP   # DISREGARD IT TO FIND MIN.
TRIAL DELINDEP WOULD EXCEED MIN BOUND
                   NEWDEL
FIRSTIME   DLOAD   DMP
                   TWEEKIT   # DLOAD TWEEKIT(40D) SENSITIVE TO
CHANGE.   PDDL   DMP   # S2(41D) SHOULDN'T CONTAIN HI ORDER

```
TARGETV          DLOAD     CALL
                 LAMENTER
                 BADR2
          SQRT   SIGN
          SR1    BOV           # SCALE BACK DOWN TO NORMAL
                 COMMNOUT
                 INFINAPO
INFINAPO  DLOAD     GOTO          # RETURNS WITH APOAPSIS IN MPAC,


          2DEC   .203966 E-8 B+28 # 1/MUM
          2DEC* 2.21422176 E4 B-15*   # SQRT(MUM)
          2DEC* .45162595 E-4 B+14*   # 1/SQRT(MUM)
# GEOMSGN  ERASE  +0
# GUESSW              # 0 IF COGA GUESS AVAILABLE, 1 IF NOT
# COGA           ERASE  +1    # INPUT ONLY IF GUESS IS ZERO.
# 0 IF UN TO BE COMPUTED, 1 IF UN INPUT
# ONLY USED IF NORMSW IS 1


# ONLY USED IF GUESSW IS 0
# AVAILABLE ONLY IF VTARGTAG IS ZERO.
# V1VEC          EQUALS   MPAC
# DEBRIS --
# RTNTR          EQUALS   RTNLAMB
# RTNAPSE  EQUALS      RTNLAMB
# SCNRDOT  ERASE  +0
# RDESIRED ERASE  +1


# ITERATOR SUBROUTINE
# ORDERSW
MAX       EQUALS      14D           # CLOBBERS 1/MU
MIN       EQUALS      8D
TWEEKIT        EQUALS     40D
# MORE KEPLER
# MORE LAMBERT
# EPSILONL EQUALS   EPSILONT +2     # DOUBLE PRECISION WORD
```

```
#     ASTRONAUT REQUEST THRU DSKY
#     (1)  SOI MANEUVER
#          DURING THE TRANSFER FROM TIG TO TIME OF INTERCEPT
#          (C)  DELTAR  THE DESIRED SEPARATION OF THE TWO VEHICLES
#          (D)  DELTTIME      THE TIME REQUIRED TO TRAVERSE DELTA R
#                        TRAVELING AT A VELOCITY EQUAL TO THE
#                        VELOCITY OF THE PASSIVE VEHICLE - SAVED FROM
#          (E)  TINT    TIME OF INTERCEPT (SOI) - SAVED FROM SOI PHASE

#                       (FOR SOI ONLY)
#     (5)  POSTTPI PERIGEE ALTITUDE OF ACTIVE VEHICLE ORBIT AFTER
#                       THE SOI (SOR) MANEUVER
#     (6)  DELVTPI MAGNITUDE OF DELTA V AT SOI (SOR) TIME
#     (7)  DELVTPF MAGNITUDE OF DELTA V AT INTERCEPT TIME
#     (8)  DELTA   VELOCITY AT SOI (AND SOR) - LOCAL VERTICAL
#     AVFLAGA      #    AVFLAGP     #    GOTOPOOH
#     BLANKET      #    ENDOFJOB    #    MAINRTNE


PREC/TT
UPDATFLG
          CALL
                    PREC/TT
          SET    DAD
          BOFF   DLOAD
                 OPTNSW
                 OPTN2


          CALL
                    S3435.25
TEST3979 BOFF     BON
                 P39/79SW
#     ASTRONAUT REQUEST THRU DSKY
#                   SAVED FROM P38/P78
#     (1)  TRKMKCNT     NUMBER OF MARKS
#     (2)  TTOGO    TIME TO GO
```

```
# OTHER VEHICLE ACTIVE
                    EXTEND
            DCA     PTIGINC
P39/P79A DXCH       KT          # TIME TO PREPARE FOR BURN
            TC      P20FLGON    # SET UPDATFLG, TRACKFLG
            TC      INTPRET
            SET     CALL
#     TIMETHET


                    OTHERV
        CALL
# Page 532
                    CSMPREC
            GOTO
                    RTRN
OTHERV              CALL
#     GOTOPOOH



VNDSPLY             EXTEND          # FLASH DISPLAY
            TS      VERBNOUN
            CA      VERBNOUN
            TCR     BANKCALL
            CADR    GOFLASH
            TCF     GOTOPOOH    # TERMINATE
            TC      RTRN        # PROCEED
            TCF     -5        # RECYCLE

V06N33SR VN         0633
V06N55SR VN         0655
V04N06SR VN         0406
V06N57SR VN         0657
V06N34SR VN         0634
V06N58SR VN         0658
V06N81SR VN         0681
# *** END OF COMEKISS.020 ***
```

PLANETARY INERTIAL ORIENTATION

PLANETARY INERTIAL ORIENTATION
***** RP-TO-R SUBROUTINE *****
SUBROUTINE TO CONVERT RP (VECTOR IN PLANETARY COORDINATE SYSTEM, EITHER
EARTH-FIXED OR MOON-FIXED) TO R (SAME VECTOR IN BASIC REF. SYSTEM)
R = MT(T) * (RP + LP X RP)   MT = M MATRIX TRANSPOSE
CALLING SEQUENCE
L   CALL

SUBROUTINES USED
EARTHMX, MOONMX, EARTHL
ITEMS AVAILABLE FROM LAUNCH DATA
504LM = THE LIBRATION VECTOR L OF THE MOON AT TIME
TIMSUBL, EXPRESSED
IN THE MOON-FIXED COORD. SYSTEM   RADIANS B0
ITEMS NECESSARY FOR SUBR. USED (SEE DESCRIPTION OF SUBR.)
MPAC = 0 FOR EARTH, NON-ZERO FOR MOON

```
          CALL                # COMPUTE M MATRIX FOR MOON
                  MOONMX        # LP=LM FOR MOONRADIANS B0
RPTORA            CALL        # EARTH COMPUTATIONS
                  EARTHMX     # M MATRIX B-1
          CALL
                  EARTHL      # L VECTOR RADIANS B0
          MXV     VSL1    # LP=M(T)*L    RAD B-0
                  MMATRIX
```

SUBROUTINE TO CONVERT R (VECTOR IN REFERENCE COORD. SYSTEM) TO RP
CALLING SEQUENCE
```
R-TO-RP           STQ    BHIZ
                  RPREXIT
                  RTORPA
          CALL
                  MOONMX
          VLOAD        VXM
```

```
                GOTO
                RPREXIT
RTORPA          CALL                 # EARTH COMPUTATIONS
                EARTHMX
        CALL
                EARTHL
                GOTO        # MPAC=L=(-AX,-AY,0)     RAD B-0
                RTORPB


                AZO
                WEARTH
        PUSH    CALL
                NEWANGLE
        SETPD   PUSH    # 18-19D=504AZ
                18D     #                   COS(AZ)   SIN(AZ)      0
        COS     PDDL    # 20-37D=  MMATRIX=   -SIN(AZ)   COS(AZ)
0    B-1


DCOMP           PDDL
                504AZ
        COS     PDVL
                HI6ZEROS
        PDDL    PUSH
                HIDPHALF
        GOTO
                EARTHMXX
```

AVECTR	=	20D	# 6	A VECTOR (MOON)
BVECTR	=	26D	# 6	B VECTOR (MOON)
504F	= 6D		# 2	**F(MOON)**

```
NODDOT      2DEC  -.457335121 E-2   # REVS/CSEC B+28=-1.07047011
NODIO       2DEC   .986209434    # REVS B-0   = 6.19653663041   RAD
FSUBO     2DEC .829090536    # REVS B-0 = 5.20932947829   RAD
BSUBO       2DEC   .0651201393    # REVS B=0   = 0.40916190299 RAD
WEARTH    2DEC .973561595    # REVS/CSEC B+23= 7.29211494 E-5  RAD/SEC
```

```
#              DESIRED ATTITUDE IS AS STORED AT L.O.
#    B) FROM RPSTART TO POLYSTOP (APPROX. +10 TO +133SECS AFTER LO)
#              DESIRED ATTITUDE IS SPECIFIED BY CMC PITCH AND ROLL
#        POLYNOMIALS DURING SATURN ROLLOUT AND PITCHOVER
#              THE DISPLAY IS RUN AS LOW PRIORITY JOB APPROX.
#              EVERY 1/2 SEC OR LESS AND IS DISABLED UPON OVFLO OF
# SUBROUTINES CALLED
#    CLEANDSP  DANZIG


# ASTRONAUT REQUESTS (IF ALTITUDE ABOVE 300,000 FT)
#    IF ASTRONAUT HAS REQUESTED ANY OF THESE DISPLAYS HE MUST
# HIT PROCEED TO RETURN TO NORMAL NOUN 62 DISPLAY.
#    ASTRONAUT  VERB 37 ENTER 00 ENTER
# ERASABLE INITIALIZATION
#    CLEAR ERADFLAG
# DEBRIS
#    BODY1, BODY2, BODY3


DXCH -PHASE5              # INACTIVE GROUP 5, PRELAUNCH PROTECTION
P11+7      EXTEND

           LAUNCHAZ
       DAD     PDDL
       TCF     +2         # CANNOT GET HERE
   TC  POSTJUMP
       CADR    NORMLIZE   # DO NORMLIZE AND ENDOFJOB
   TCF REP11A      -5     # T2,T1 NOT YET ZEROED, GO AND DO IT


ATERTASK   CAF    PRIO1   # ESTABLISH JOB TO DISPLAY ATT ERRORS
           TC     FINDVAC           # COMES HERE AT L.O. + .33 SEC
           EBANK=    BODY3
           2CADR     ATERJOB
           CS     RCSFLAGS # SET BIT3 FOR
           MASK   BIT3     # NEEDLER
           TC     TASKOVER
GETDOWN       STQ    SETPD
```

```
            TC      ENDOFJOB    # STAURN STICK ON -- KILL JOB
            CAF     BIT10       # CHECK IF S/C CONTROL
    CCS     SATSW               # IT IS NOT -- WAS IT ON LAST CYCLE
            DAD     DSU         # ASSUMING X(SM) ALONG LAUNCH AZIMUTH,
            PUSH                # LET R(RAD) = 2*PI*ROLL(REV)
            SIN     PUSH
            PUSH    CALL        #       MGC     OGC
            DAD     SR2         # CHANGE SCALE OF AK TO 2REVS

            GOTO
            DMP     PUSH
            DAD     SL1
            TC      ATERJOB         # END OF ATT ERROR DISPLAY CYCLE
TAKEON      CAF     BIT9        # ENABLE
                AMOONFLG
EARTHALT    BDSU
            EXTEND                  # IS COMPLETED

            EXTEND
            EXTEND                  # ROLLOUT COMPLETED
#   ASTRONAUT MAY REQUEST SATURN TAKEOVER THROUGH
#   EXTENDED VERB 46 (BITS 13,14 OF DAPDATR1 SET ).
#   COMMANDS AND IT TRANSMITS THESE TO SATURN AS DC
#   VOLTAGES.  THE VALUE OF THE CONSTANT RATE COMMAND
#   IS 0.5 DEG/SEC.  AN ABSENCE OF RHC ACTIVITY RE-
#   VERB 46 ENTER       (SEE ASTRONAUT ABOVE)

            CADR    ZEROJET         # LEAVE THE T6 CLOCK DISABLED
            SBANK=      LOWSUPER
            SETLOC          P11FOUR
            QXCH    QRUPT
            RXOR    CHAN31          # CHECK IF MAN ROT BITS SAME
            CADR    STICKCHK    # FOR PITCH YAW AND ROLL
            CADR    NEEDLER
            TCF     RESUME          # END OF SATURN STICK CONTROL
```

```
# Filename:INTERPRETER.agc


DANZIG          CA     BANKSET                      # SET BBANK BEFORE
DIRADRES   INDEX LOC                      # LOOK AHEAD TO NEXT WORD TO SEE
           NOOP
           MASK   HIGH4                 # IF ADDRESS GREATER THAN 2K,
           EXTEND
           ADS    ADDRWD                # DO AUGMENT, IGNORING AND
# LIST.   IN MOST CASES THE MODE OF THE RESULT (VECTOR OR SCALAR) OF
THE LAST ARITHMETIC OPERATION PERFORMED

# IS THE SAME AS THE TYPE OF OPERAND DESIRED (ALL ADD/SUBTRACT ETC.).
EXCEPTIONS TO THIS GENERAL RULE ARE LISTED
#             RESULT, VXSC WANTS A SCALAR.
           MASK   CYR     # 20, THIS OP REQUIRES SPECIAL ATTENTION.
           INDEX  A       # NO -- THE MODE IS DEFINITE.  PICK UP THE
           TCF    UNAJUMP      # 1-4 OF A (ZERO, EXIT, HAS BEEN
           TCF    DAD     # 34 -- DP ADD.
           TCF    LXA     # 02 -- LOAD INDEX FROM ERASABLE.


# THE FOLLOWING JUMP TABLE APPLIES TO UNARY INSTRUCTIONS
           MASK   LOW8
# SSP (STORE SINGLE PRECISION) IS EXECUTED HERE.
SSP        INCR   LOC     # PICK UP THE WORD FOLLOWING THE GIVEN
           EBANK=    1400         # SO YUL DOESN'T CUSS THE "CA 1400"
           READ   LCHAN        # DCA 0 OR DCS 0
DAD        EXTEND
SETOVF        TC  OVERFLOW


OVERFLWZ   TS     L       # ENTRY FOR THIRD COMPONENT.
OVERFLWY   TS     L       # ENTRY FOR SECOND COMPONENT.
OVERFLOW   INDEX  A       # ENTRY FOR 1ST COMP OR DP (L=0).
           TC     Q       # NO OVERFLOW EXIT.
           TCF    NEWMODE
# THE FOLLOWING IS THE PROLOGUE TO V/SC.  IF THE PRESENT MODE IS
VECTOR, IT SAVES THE SCALAR AT X IN BUF
SHORTT          CAF    SIX        # SCALAR SHORT SHIFTS COME HERE.
```

```
TSSR          INDEX SR        # GET SHIFTING BIT.
              CCS   CYR       # SEE IF A ROUND IS DESIRED.
RIGHTR              TC  MPACSRND   # YES -- SHIFT RIGHT AND ROUND.
              TS    MPAC +2       # AND ROUND.)
# ROUTINE FOR SHORT SCALAR SHIFT LEFT (AND MAYBE ROUND).
              CA    MPTEMP        # SEE IF SHIFT COUNT LESS THAN 14D.
              BZMF  VSSR      # IF SO, BRANCH AND SHIFT IMMEDIATELY.
              TC    SETROUND  # X COMPONENT NOW SHIFTED, SO MAKE UP


SMPAC+              AD   -1/2+2           # SEE IF ARGUMENT GREATER
              DXCH  MPAC      # WE WILL TAKE THE SQUARE ROOT OF
ARGHI         CAF   SLOPEHI       # ARGUMENT BETWEEN .25 AND .5, GET
              AD    BIASHI        # X0/2 = (MPAC/2)(SLOPHI) + BIASHI/2.
ARGLO               CAF   SLOPELO       # (NORMALIZED) ARGUMENT
              AD    BIASLO
              EXTEND              # IF SO, WE LOST (OR GAINED) PI, SO
              DOUBLE              # MAGNITUDE.  IF SO, REDUCE IT TO


              DOUBLE
              TCF   ACOSST        # START IMMEDIATELY IF POSITIVE.
ACOSST              CS    HALF    # TEST MAGNITUDE OF INPUT.
              TCF   ACOSOVF       # THIS IS PROBABLY AN OVERFLOW
              TC    ESCAPE
              CCS   MPTEMP        # SEE IF UN-NORMALIZATION
              CAF   LBUF2         # DO FINAL MULTIPLY AND GO TO ANY
LDANZIG             TCF   DANZIG


ACOSOVF             EXTEND                # IF MAJOR PART WAS ONLY 1
ACOSABRT      TC    ALARM         # IF OVERFLOW, CALL ANSWER ZERO
              INDEX FIXLOC        # SLOW IN THIS CASE, BUT SAVES
# THE ADDRESS ITSELF IS MADE UP BY THE YUL SYSTEM ASSEMBLER
              EXTEND              # DISPATCH SWITCH BIT OPERATION
              TS    STATE         # NEW SWITCH WORD.
              MP    POLISH        # CODE.
    +13D      TCF   DANZIG        # 11 -- NOOP.
```

Mod history: 2009-05-13 RSB Adapted from the Colossus249/ **file of**
the same name, using Comanche055 page images.

DEBRIS....
MUCH, SHAREABLE WITH RCS/ENTRY, IN EBANK6 ONLY
PITCH TVCDAP STARTS HERE....(INCOPORATES CSM/LEM DAP FILTER, **MODOR**

```
PITCHDAP   LXCH   BANKRUPT   # T5 ENTRY, NORMAL OR VIA DAPINIT
PSTROKER   CCS    STROKER       # (STRKFLG) CHECK FOR STROKE TEST
           TC     HACK       # TEST-START OR TEST-IN-PROGRESS
           TCF    +2         # NO-TEST
           TC     HACK       # TEST-IN-PROGRESS


PCDUDOTS   CAE    CDUY       # COMPUTE CDUYDOT (USED BY PITCH AND
YAW)
           EXTEND
           TCR    RLIMTEST   #   RATE TEST
           CAE    CDUZ       # COMPUTE CDUZDOT (USED BY PITCH AND
           EXTEND
RLIMTEST   TS     TTMP1         # TEST FOR EXCESSIVE CDU RATES
(GREATER


PERIOD
           EXTEND
PINTEGRL   EXTEND                # COMPUTE INTEGRAL OF BODY-AXIS
PITCH-RATE
           DCA    PERRB      #   ERROR, SC.AT B-1 REVS
           CS     COSCDUZ      # PREPARE BODY-AXIS PITCH RATE,
OMEGAYB
           MP     COSCDUX


           EXTEND                # PICK UP -OMEGAYB (SIGN CHNG,
PERORLIM   TCR    ERRORLIM   # PITCH BODY-AXIS-ERROR INPUT LIMITER
PFORWARD   EXTEND             #    PREPARE THE FILTER STORAGE
           TCR    FWDFLTR    # GO COMPUTE PRESENT OUTPUT
                             # (INCLUDES VARIABLE GAIN PACKAGE)
POFFSET           EXTEND
POUT       CS     PCMD       # INCREMENTAL PITCH COMMAND
                             #    PROTECT. SINCE ERROR CNTR ZEROED)
```

```
            CAF     BIT11       # BIT FOR TVCPITCH COUNT RELEASE
PCOPY       INCR    TVCPHASE    # RESTART-PROTECT THE COPYCYCLE. (1)
                                #   PACKAGE, SHOULD A RESTART OCCUR
            DXCH    PERRB
            CAE     CMDTMP         #   PITCH ACTUATOR COMMAND
# YAW TVCDAP STARTS HERE....(INCORPORATES CSM/LEM DAP FILTER, MODOR
YAWDAP              LXCH    BANKRUPT # T5 ENTRY, NORMAL
            QXCH    QRUPT


            AUTOPILOT (LOW-
YERORLIM    TCR     ERRORLIM    # YAW BODY-AXIS-ERROR INPUT LIMITER
            ADS     TVCYAW         # UPDATE THE ERROR COUNTER (NO
# SUBROUTINES COMMON TO BOTH PITCH AND YAW DAPS....
            MASK    BIT14
            TCF     3DAPCAS        # LEM ON
            EXTEND              # (ALSO, SIGN CHANGE IN FORWARD
            MP      VARK        # SCALED AT 1/(8 ASCREV) OF ACTUAL VALUE


                                # NOTE -- THERE IS AN INHERENT GAIN OF
            CS      DAP1  +1    # MULTIPLY OUTPUT BY
            EXTEND                   # SECOND-ORDER NUMERATOR COEFF.
            CS      DAP1  +1    # MULTIPLY OUTPUT BY
            MP      N10   +4    #  D12
            CS      DAP1
            MP      N10   +4    #  D12
2CASFLTR    CAF     ZERO        # **** SECOND CASCADE FILTER **********

            CA      DAP1  +1    # MULTIPLY INPUT BY
            CS      DAP2  +1    # MULTIPLY OUTPUT BY
            CAE     DAPDATR1    # TEST FOR LEM ON OR OFF
            TC      Q           # EXIT IF LEM OFF
            EXTEND
            EXTEND
            EXTEND
DAPT5       GENADR  DAPINIT              #(BBCON) ALREADY THERE.
```

Part Three:
Moonbit: The 64 Bit Poem Breakdown

Anglfind

Pick up angles
compute mis compute
from final to stable

transpose proceed calculate Dad
Checkmax exit hint
direct CS One nogo will stop good return

go max load
am maxang vload
altcalc unit skew store is the maneuver

if I am greater than
scale $ root 2 $root2 $root
large adjust accordingly

locskirt   ocskirt   sign of cskirt
matrix operations multiplies and leaves
define skirt

push go to matrix enter
return minang maxang lock contants
avoid divisions by zero

sin $2 sin $2
cos $2 cos $2
sin(ngl)cos(d)

$2 read hint
with the current
logic the sin

scaled star
where u is a unit a is the angle
Dad complement will be left terminating #goodend

Body Attitude

Provide a stable un end of the phase quit
load branch same uya in olduya
store old uya or save as case may be
finish obtaining trajectory triad

is ok, go on
come here

this assumes that the name is not changed
ignore gam if leq
tag if too small
come here   hint

gov correct if any
roll single
get double
same as needed for dop   e   extend

re-starts come here
can't danzig
after phaschng
return store magic pop

limit costs 2 r re red

Conic Subroutines

Solve various problems produced by a force
acting on a general usage point-of-view
only one set of coding is used

the earth, moon, or any other celestial body
interrupt each other. It is up to the user
Colossus 103 and Sundance 222 (August 1968)

Desire updated trajectory may be
circular, elliptical, parabolic, hyperbolic, or rectilinear
respect to the earth or the moon

dad desired time
debris may be of use
lamb push fin slope

function true-anomaly-difference
circle, ellipse, parabola, or hyperbola
with respect to the earth or the moon

Firstime boff
disregard trial would exceed newdel
firstime sensitive to change.

Hi
Call lamenter
bad sign

scaled back down
commnout infinapo
returns

/MUM   (MUM)   SQRT(MUM)
Erase guess if guess is zero
if input norm

only used if guessw is 0
if vtargtag is zero
equals debris lamb la   b

erase desire iterator orders
clobber equals tweekit
more kepler more lambert equals double precision

Stable Orbit

Astronaut request soi maneuver
from tig to time

deltar the desired
the time required

to traverse delta
equal to the saved

for the soi (sor) maneuver
magnitude time

magnitude of flag
flag   gotop00h blanket

call dad boff dload
call boff bon

astronaut request thru dsky
Saved from marks

time to go
time to prepare for burn

call meth
call other

gotop00h proceed recycle
End of comekiss

Planetary Inertial Orientation

Either Earth-fixed or Moon-fixed
matrix transpose calling L
EarthMx, MoonMx, EarthL
the libration of the moon expressed
0 for Earth, non-zero for Moon
compute M matrix for Moon
MoonMX Moonraidans
#Earth computations EarthMX
reference sequence bhiz
rprexit call moonmx
vload rprexit call #Earth computations
EarthMX call EarthL WEarth push call
Newangle push goto Earth
Avectr Bvectr F(Moon) NoDio WEarth

Desire after desire
During Saturn rollout and pitchover
run as low priority
disabled called danzig

astronaut requests he must return to normal
astronaut erasable
clear debris
Body1, Body2, Body3

Prelaunch protection
P11 + 7
launchaz Dad
cannot get here
postjump normlize
go and do it

aftertask find Body3
mask task getdown

kill job
check if
it is not - was it on last cycle Dad
push push push Dad

Goto push Dad
error display cycle
takeon
amoonflg
earthalt

extend extend extend
astronaut may request Saturn takeover

extended verb 46
it transmits
the value of absence
see astronaut above

Zerojet leave the clock disabled
lowsuper p11four Qrupt
check if man rot bits same
for pitch
yaw
and roll

needle
end of control

Interpreter

Danzig look ahead
to next word
to see noop
mask high4 extend
augment the result
last arithmetic
The general wants a mask
requires special attention
No—the mode is definite
pick up the unajump
dad erasable
the following jump
low8 is executed here
pick up the word
so YUL doesn't cuss
read Dad extend overflow
Overflwz Overflwy Overflow index
no exit newmode
the following in the prologue
it saves short shifts
come here
I get a round
desired right and round and round
and maybe round
shift and make up
if argument greater
we will take the square root
arghi slopehi biashi
arglo slopelo biaslo
if so, we lost
if so, reduce it to double
acosst start immediately acosst
half this is probably an escape
un-normalization

go to Danzig
Extend major alarm
slow in this case, but saves
the YUL system assembler
dispatch switch bit
state new switch word
polish code Danzig

File of the Same Name

Debris…much, shareable
Pitch TVCDAP Starts Here…Modor
PitchDap Bankrupt Stroker

Hack
Test-start Test-in-progress No-test
Hack

By pitch and yaw extend
Rate test compute extend
Test for excessive greater period extend

Pintegrl pitch-rate SC.AT
Prepare body OMEGAYB COSCDUX
Pick up sign Body-Axis-Error

Pforward Fwdfltr
Go compute present output
Include Poffsett Pout Protect

Bit for TVCpitch
Protect the Copy
Should a restart occur

Perrb Pitch starts here
Bankrupt Normal
Qrupt Autopilot (Low-

Yerorlim Errorlim
Update the error
Common to both pitch and yaw daps

Bit lem on
Also, vark
There is an inherent gain of dap

Second-order numerator
By D12 Dap D12
Cascade

Multiply input by
Multiply output by
On or off Q exit if

Extend extend extend
Dapinit
Already there.

R00003

Code Poetics

"The practitioner of literate programming can be regarded as an essayist, whose main concern is with exposition and excellence of style."
—Donald Knuth, "Literate Programming"

Despite the limitations of the AGC code, which range from the concise syntax of Yul and AGC's extended yet still restricted interpretive language, the small amount of punch card space available for use in coding each line, and the requirement of a compact body of instructions, the AGC code contains a wealth of imaginative and highly creative language. Some of the wordplay found in the AGC code resembles what John A. Barry calls "technobabble": specific technological metaphors invented to describe and explain computing that are also frequently used to describe human behaviors in computing terms.[1] But there are also references and riffs on popular culture, contemporary political events, and other textual sources. Perhaps in acknowledgment of the poverty of the system's vocabulary, the AGC programmers filled the code with rich, descriptive language and cultural and literary references. We can find playful use of language from the most visible elements of the system, the main astronaut interface to the computer, to one of the most hidden components, the use of extended literary quotes within the remarks section of the code that would never even be processed and interpreted by the assembling programs.

One of the major innovations of the Apollo Guidance Computer project was the development of what was essentially real-time computing. In a 2001 group interview with other MIT Instrumentation Lab AGC programmers, Albrecht "Alex" Kosmala remarked on the incredulity he experiences when he explains to programmers that this "real-time control computer with an event-driven, asynchronous executive" was developed in the 1960s.[2] The AGC needed to quickly respond to input from instruments and the astronaut interface. Rather than operating in a synchronous fashion, meaning the linear completion of one computational task after another, the programmers wanted to design a system that could very quickly shift from the execution of one job to another. The implementation of this system required the addition of a significant amount of code but it made possible both the asynchronous execution and a powerful form of error recovery. The "executive" referenced by Kosmala is a distinct program and the major enabling technology for these advanced functions. The EXECUTIVE program's respon-

1   John A. Barry, *Technobabble* (Cambridge: MIT Press, 1991), xiii
2   "Innovations in Software," *Apollo Guidance Computer History Project: Second Conference*, September 14, 2001, https://authors.library.caltech.edu/5456/1/hrst.mit.edu/hrs/apollo/public/conference2/innovations.htm.

sibility is to run jobs and to make sure that it is always running the job with the highest priority.

The EXECUTIVE combined with another program called WAITLIST, which managed the queue of smaller bits of code called tasks, provided the AGC with the ability to interrupt and resume execution of programs. Together WAITLIST and EXECUTIVE provided essentially what we call an operating system for the AGC. The WAITLIST program is dated in the code as being written on October 10, 1966 and modified four times. The following is slightly reformatted code from the scanned images:

```
L WAITLIST
R0001 PROGRAM DESCRIPTION              DATE -- 10 OCTOBER 1966
R0003 MOD NO -- 2             LOG SECTION -- WAITLIST
R0005 MOD BY -- MILLER        (DTMAX INCREASED TO 162.5 SEC)
                ASSEMBLY -- SUNBURST REV 5
R00072 MOD 3 BY KERNAN  (INHINT INSERTED AT WAITLIST) 2/28/68 SKIPPER REV 4
R00073 MOD 4 BY KERNAN  (TWIDDLE IN 54) 3/28/68 SKIPPER REV 13.
R000799
```

This code listing shows that there were major and minor modifications of the code as a whole and that these major modifications involved a renumber. The modification that introduced MOD 3 on February 28, 1968 was most likely part of the same major modification as MOD 4 on March 28, 1968, as the added cards (R00072 and R00073) were not renumbered. MOD 3 introduced inhibited interrupt (INHINT) mode during WAITLIST, ensuring that tasks run through the WAITLIST were executed to completion. WAITLIST was used, as the code reads, TO CALL A PROGRAM (CALLED A TASK). It had a limited list of nine tasks that could be in the queue or task list. If the length of tasks exceeded the maximum number, the program executes (in other words, TCF or transfers control) the following routine, called WTABORT:

```
WTABORT    TC     FILLED
           NOOP   # CAN'T GET HERE
           AD     ONE
           TC     WTLST2
           OCT 10
...
FILLED     DXCH   WAITEXIT
       TC BAILOUT1 # NO ROOM IN THE INN
       OCT  01203
```

WTABORT, again, executes another instruction, this one called FILLED, that eventually "bails" out of the program and produces an alarm state. The code in this section is concerned with error states and how to address the problem of running out of space, of not having any rooms in the inn. There are checks to make sure that there is truly a "no vacancy" or FILLED state before generating an alarm. The WAITLIST "tasks" were required to be short running – they could run from 0.01 seconds (a centisecond) to 162.5 seconds – and thus much of the code for this program concerns waiting, counting time, and the timing of the tasks.

The AGC, however, did have some basic interrupt and restart features in the form of restart protection prior to the addition of the EXECUTIVE. Restart protection depended upon the existence of restart points stored in erasable memory that could survive power loss. These restart or checkpoints were scattered throughout the code at crucial points. When the AGC was restarted, it resumed execution at the restarted point, restoring the previous saved state. Restarts could be forced by software – a feature part of many contemporary operating systems known as a kernel panic – in order to protect from overloading and potential corruption of data. We can see an example of this in Don Eyles's explanation of the origin of an oddly named instruction known as WHIMPER that appears as such in the Apollo 11 AGC code:

```
WHIMPER    CA       TWO
           AD       Z
           TS       BRUPT
           RESUME
           TC       POSTJUMP      # RESUME SENDS CONTROL HERE
           CADR     ENEMA
```

In a previous version of the code, Eyles explains, WHIMPER appeared in a simple form with a playful and somewhat helpful remark: "The instruction at tag WHIMPER transferred control to the instruction at TAG WHIMPER, whereupon TC Trap would detect the endless loop and trigger the restart."[3] The line, according to Eyles, appeared as such prior to the Luminary 1A build 099 that was used in the Apollo 11 flight:

```
WHIMPER    TC       WHIMPER       NOT WITH A BANG....
```

The remark included in this earlier code quotes, within the designated remark space of the card, part of the final line of T.S. Eliot's 1925 poem "The Hollow Men," which was preceded by "This is the way the world ends." The AGC programmers allude to these lines in their naming of the condition of a forced restart by the TC Trap job. The TC Trap job monitored the progress of other programs and was capable of initiating a software (rather than hardware) restart to reestablish a known state for the AGC. The programmers explicitly referred to this procedure — an innovation in computer systems design — as a software restart. Calling the WHIMPER instruction triggers an endlessly looping recursive state which would necessitate a restart — the end of the world for the computer, but much better than a possible "bang" as a result of an unrecoverable and undetected error or an inoperable AGC. Following the revision of the WHIMPER function to no longer produce the self-referential trap condition and the removal of the no-longer relevant remark, the name stuck "for sentimental reasons" without any markers to indicate the original referent. WHIMPER remained in the code as the name of the subroutine used as part of a software restart.

3   Don Eyles, *Sunburst and Luminary: An Apollo Memoir* (Boston: Four Point Press, 2018), 82.

Far less disruptive to the operation of AGC than a TC Trap software-initiated restart was the normal process of interruption used by the EXECUTIVE program. The AGC programmer's manual describes the process of interruption:

> This means that the normal sequence of instructions of a program may be broken into at any point, and that control is transferred to some other program. There is a short subroutine which has the net effect of returning control to the original (interrupted) program, with no loss of information if certain precautions are taken.[4]

The occurrence of an interrupt signal stops or breaks the execution of currently running programs to run a program with a higher priority. These occur frequently and are what makes real-time computation possible. The notion of an interrupt has found widespread adoption in computing to enable multitasking, quick responses to events and triggers, and to address the common problem of input devices running at much slower speeds than processors. The EXECUTIVE program continuously runs an idling program or subroutine known as DUMMYJOB. This subroutine has the lowest priority, thus making sure that will only be executed when nothing else needs to be computed.

```
DUMMYJOB     CS       ZERO        # SET NEWJOB TO -0 FOR IDLING.
             TS       NEWJOB
             RELINT
             CS       TWO         # TURN OFF THE ACTIVITY LIGHT.
             EXTEND
             WAND     DSALMOUT
```

The DUMMYJOB instruction is introduced with a remark that explains that the idling process "is not a job in itself, but rather a subroutine of the executive." If there are no jobs running, the DUMMYJOB subroutine is executed, turning off the activity light and making sure that the EXECUTIVE is available for running any jobs. In turning off the activity light, the AGC alerts the astronaut that the system is idling, running DUMMYJOB. In the above code, we

---

4   Ramon Alonso, J. Halcombe Laning, Jr., and Hugh Blair-Smith, *E-1077: Preliminary MOD 3C Programmers Manual* (Cambridge: MIT Instrumentation Laboratory, 1961), 17.

see the instruction RELINT called. This instruction enables interrupts and is generally used in combination with INHINT, an instruction that inhibits interrupt activity for brief and important tasks that cannot be safely interrupted. The instruction TC RIP is used to Transfer Control to Resume Interrupted Program, which restarts the preserved state of the prior program.

Military-style acronyms fill the world of the Apollo mission and many make their way into the code. Short and concise, these acronyms compress language into the smallest amount of space required to communicate a concept. Acronyms were also particularly well suited to the computational environment because these computers and the devices used to input and store the code, the punch card systems, all had limited space and required the use of capital letters. Much of the wordplay appearing in the code turns on the ambiguities and slipperiness of these otherwise precise, short terms. The Lunar Module was abbreviated everywhere in the code as LM, which was always pronounced as "Lim." The main input device for operating the guidance computer was called the "Display and Keyboard." This name was shortened to DSKY, which the programmers and astronauts pronounced as "Diskey," which Don Eyles explains was pronounced to rhyme with whiskey.[5]

The program that was responsible for handling the DSKY user interface — in other words, responding to the astronaut's manual input and displaying output values, alarms, and present system status — was playfully named PINBALL GAME BUTTONS AND LIGHTS. The DSKY was operated by entering a two-digit "verb" to perform an action on another two-digit object or "noun." A set of remarks in the code explains the logic behind this mode of communication with the computer:

```
# THE LANGUAGE OF COMMUNICATION WITH THE PROGRAM IS A PAIR OF WORDS
# KNOWN AS VERB AND NOUN.  EACH OF THESE IS REPRESENTED BY A 2 CHARACTER
# DECIMAL NUMBER.  THE VERB CODE INDICATES WHAT ACTION IS TO BE TAKEN, THE
# NOUN CODE INDICATES TO WHAT THIS ACTION IS APPLIED.  NOUNS USUALLY
# REFER TO A GROUP OF ERASABLE REGISTERS.
```

On the far left side of the DSKY were the VERB and NOUN buttons. On the far right, ENTR and RSET. To operate the DSKY, to perform some task, the astronaut pressed VERB and then entered the two-digit program number, then pressed

5   Eyles, *Sunburst and Luminary*, 47.

NOUN, followed by the two-digit code for the action, and finally pressed enter or ENTR. The use of a NOUN was not always required; some programs would be run with just a VERB. **Figure 5** shows an image of the summary card with the NOUN and VERB list used for a subsequent version of the AGC. The language of nouns and verbs, one of the most simple yet flexible user interfaces that one can imagine, can be found throughout the code. This is a compact but powerful method of interaction that continues to present in the inverted form of selection (noun) and clicking (noun) in graphical user interfaces.

Despite its functional design imperative and the limited syntax of the Yul programming language, we find a real sense of humor and play within the AGC code. Perhaps this is because all authors and programmers, when exploiting the few given freedoms available in any discourse, have a tendency toward pushing the limits of the existing language. Programming is as much of a "language game" as any other language and the tightened boundaries of a small syntax give way to a sense of play found within any constrained environment. The use of the terms "nouns" and "verbs" within both the hardware and software systems of the AGC invite a playful reading of the code as self-aware of the limits of this particular language. The stripped-down syntax invites exploration of the combination of two-digit noun and verb codes. In a section of code just below the above, in which programmers or "the authors," as they called themselves, supply lines spoken by Jack Cade in Shakespeare's *King Henry XI*.[6]

```
# THE FOLLOWING QUOTATION IS PROVIDED THROUGH THE COURTESY OF THE AUTHORS.
#
# "IT WILL BE PROVED TO THY FACE THAT THOU HAST MEN ABOUT THEE THAT
# USUALLY TALK OF A NOUN AND A VERB, AND SUCH ABOMINABLE WORDS AS NO
# CHRISTIAN EAR CAN ENDURE TO HEAR."
#                                              HENRY 6, ACT 2, SCENE 4
```

These remarks, the only quoted lines but not the only reference to Shakespeare found in the code, add some humor to the programmer's reliance on the noun and verb structure.[7] The two-digit VERB and NOUN thus provided the

---

6   Ronald S. Burkey has added a note to the code uploaded to Github with the correct citation for this passage: *King Henry VI*, Part 2, Act IV, Scene VII.
7   Hugh Blair-Smith provides his interpretation of these lines in "Annotations to Eldon Hall's *Journey to the Moon*," *Apollo Guidance Computer History Project*, February 1997,

VERB LIST

01-05	DISPLAY OCTAL
06	DISPLAY DECIMAL
07	DP DEC DSPLY (≤N38)
11-15	MONITOR OCTAL
16	MONITOR DECIMAL
17	DP DEC MON (≤N38)
21-25	LOAD DATA
27 01	DSPLY FIXED MEMORY
30	EXECUTIVE (PRE/L N26)
31	WAITLIST (PRE/L N26)
32	RECYCLE
33	PROCEED (REQ W/ V 21-V23)
34	TERMINATE (EXCEPT N49,60,63,88)
35	TEST LITES (P00)
36	FRESH START
37	CHANGE PROGRAM
40 20	ZERO ICDU'S
40 72	ZERO RR CDU'S
41 20	IMU CRS ALN
41 72	RR CRS ALN
42	GYRO TORQ
43	LOAD FDAI ERROR NEEDLES (P00)
44	TERM RR DESIGNATE
47	INITIALIZE AGS
48	DAP DATA LOAD
49	CREW ATT MNVR (P00)
50	PLEASE PERFORM
52	REQST CURSOR MK
53	REQST SPIRAL MK
54	REQST X OR Y MK
55	INCRMT CLK (H,M,S)
56	TERM TRACKING
57	PERMIT LR UPDTS
58	INHIBIT LR UPDTS
59	CMD LR TO POSN 2
60	DAP ATT RTS (ERR NDLS)
61	DAP FOLLOW ATT ERROR (MODE 1 ERR NDLS)
62	TOTAL ATT ERR (N22-N20) (MODE 2 ERR NDLS)
63	RR/LR SELF-TEST
64	S-BAND ANT (06 51)
65	DISABLE U-V JETS
66	LM SV TO CSM SLOTS
67	DSPLY W-MATRIX RSS ERROR (06 99)
68	TERM TERRAIN MODEL
69	FORCE RESTART
70	LIFTOFF TIME UPDT (P27)
71	BLOCK ADRS UPDT (P27)
72	SINGLE ADRS UPDT (P27)
73	LGC CLK OCT UPDT (P27)
74	START ERASABLE DUMP
75	ENABLE U-V JETS
76	MINIMUM IMPULSE
77	RATE CMD/ATT HOLD
78	START LR SPURIOUS TEST
79	STOP LR SPURIOUS TEST
80	UPDT LM SV (P20)
81	UPDT CSM SV (P20,P22)
82	ORBIT PMTR DSPLY(16 44)
83	RDZ PMTR DSPLY (16 54)
85	DSPLY RR LOS AZ, ELEV ∡ (16 56)
89	RDZ FNL ATT MNVR (P00)
90	RDZ OUT-OF-PLANE DSPLY (06 90)
91	DSPLY BANKSUM (P00) (BK SUM,BK,BUGGER NEXT BANK-PRO TERM-V34E)
93	ENABLE W-MATRIX INITIALIZATION
95	INHIBIT SV UPDTS (P20,P22)
96	STOP SV INTEGRATION
97	PERFORM ENGINE FAIL PROCEDURE
99	ENABLE ENGINE IGN

ROUTINE CROSS-REF

R03/V48	R36/V90
R04/V63	R47/V47
R05/V64	R56/V56
R30/V82	R62/V49
R31/V83	R63/V89
R33/V06N65	R77/V78

NOUN LIST

* - LEGIT LOADABLE NOUN & DATA VALID ANYTIME NOUN CALLED
V - DATA VALID ANYTIME NOUN CALLED
L - LEGIT LOADABLE NOUN
X - LEGIT LOADABLE NOUN (HR, MIN, .01S) (IF LOAD, ENTR R1,R2,R3)

01,02,03 * SPECIFIED OCT ADRS

DSPY	OCT	DEC
N01	[OCT]	[.XXXXX]
N02	[OCT]	[XXXXX.]
N03	[OCT]	[.01°]

04	GRAVITY ERR ∡ [.01°(R1)]
05	SIGHT ∡ DIFF/SV-RR LOS ∡[.01°(R1)]
06 L	OPTION CODE[OCT] (SEE P21, P22, P52, P57)
07 L	ADRS/CHNL,BIT ID,ACTION [OCT] (SEE "FLAGWRD/CHNL SET/RESET")
08 V	ALARM DATA[OCT] (ALMCADR, "BBCON", ERCOUNT)
09 V	ALARM CODES [OCT] (1ST, 2ND, MOST RECENT ALM)
10 *	SPECIFIED CHNL [OCT(R1)] (CAN'T 34, CAN'T 3, 4, 7,15 READ 35 LOAD 16,30,31,32 IF LOAD CH 33, RESETS BITS 15-11
11 X	T CSI OR T APOAPSIS [H,M,.01S] (0,0,0 = COMPUTE T APOAPSIS)
12 L	OPTN CODE [OCT (0000X, 0000Y)]

	X (SPFY)	Y=1	Y=2
V82	2 (VEH)	LM	CSM
V89	3 (TK ATT)	+Z	+X
V63	4 (RADAR)	RR	LR
41 72	6 (RR FN)	LOCK	DESIG

13 X	T CDH [H,M,.01S]
15 *	INCREMENTED OCT ADRS [OCT(R1)]
16 X	T EVENT [H,M,.01S] (AGSK = PRSNT IF V32E (V47) (0,0,0 = PRSNT T (V90)
18	AUTO MNVR FDAI ∡-R,P,Y [.01°]
20 V	PRSNT ICDU'S - Y,P,R [.01°]
21 V	PIPA PULSES X,Y,Z [XXXXX.]
22 L	DSRD NEW ICDU'S - Y,P,R [.01°]
24 X	LGC CLK ΔT [H,M,.01S]
25	SEE "V50 CHECKLIST" [OCT(R1,R2)]
26 *	PRIO/DELAY, ADRES, "BBCON" [OCT] (SEE V30, V31)
27 *	SELF-TEST ON/OFF SW [OCT(R1)] (START: 00010 (ALL) STOP:00000 00004(ERAS) ALSO 00005(FIXED) (V36, V91)
32	T FROM PERIGEE [H, M, .01S]
33 X	TIG [H,M,.01S]
34 X	T EVENT [H,M,.01S](0,0,0 = PRSNT T)
35	TFI/TCO [H,M,.01S]
36 V	LGC CLOCK TIME [H, M, .01S]
37 X	T TPI [H, M, .01S]
38 V	INTEG SV TIME TAG [H, M, .01S]
40	TFI/TCO,VG,ΔVM[M:S, .1FPS,.1FPS]
42	HA,HP,VG [.1NM, .1NM, .1FPS]
43	LAT,LON, ALT [.01°, .01°, .1NM] (+N, +E, + > RLS)
44	HA,HP,TFF [.1NM, .1NM, M:S] (TFF = -59 59 IF HP > 35K FT)
45 V/R1	MKS, TFI, +MGA [X., M:S, .01°] (R3=-0001: NOT FINAL R3=-00002: P7X OR FNL, NO ALN R3=+MGA: FNL,IMU ALN
46 L	DAP CONFG,CHANBKUP[OCT(R1,R2)] (CONFG: SEE "DAP DATA LOAD" (CHANBKUP: IGNORE SPFY DSCRT 00001 - ABORT/ABORT STAGE 00010 - AUTO THRTL 00011 - BOTH DSCRTS
47 *	LM WT, CSM WT [LBM (R1), R2)]
48 L	DPS P,R GMBL TRIM [.01°(R1,R2)]
49	ΔR, ΔV, SOURCE [.01NM, .1FPS, X.] (X=1 RANGE X=3 SHFT X=2 RNG RT X=4 TRUN)
51	DSRD S-BAND P, Y ∡ [.01°(R1, R2)]
52	ACT VEH CENTRL ∡[.01°(R1)] (AVOID 170° - 190° REGION)
54	RANGE, RDOT(- CLOSE),+Z/HORZ ∡ [.01NM, .1FPS, .01°]
55 L	P32: APSIS, ELEV, CODE [X.,.01°, Y] (Y=0: CDH AT APSIS SPFY BY R1) (Y≠0: CDH AT (R1)x(180°) L P34: CODE, ELEV, TRANSFER ∡ [X.,.01°,.01°] (X=0 CONIC ELEV= 0 T OPTN) (X≠0 ENCKE ELEV= 0 ∡ OPTN)
56	RR LOS AZ, ELEV [.01°(R1, R2)] (AZ +/LM Z, ELEV +/Y)
58	PREDICT POST-TPI HP, TPI ΔV, TPF ΔV [.1NM, .1FPS, .1FPS]
59	LOS ΔV VEC (FWD, RT, DN IF BORE ⊀, IN-PLANE, HEADS-UP) [.1FPS]
60	VI(+Z), HDOT(-/HI), H [.1FPS, .1FPS, FT]
61	TG (AIM PT), TFI, XR (+/LS N) [M:S, M:S, .1NM]
62	VI, TFI, ΔVM [.1FPS, M:S, .1FPS]
63	ΔH (LR-PGNS), HDOT (-/HI), H [FT, .1FPS, FT]
64	TR:LPD, HDOT(-/HI), H [S.°, .1FPS, FT]
65 V	SAMPLED LGC TIME [H, M, .01S] (IF LGC/CMC CLK SYNC) (V06N65...E, SYNC W/ CMP) (V55 ΔT = CSM T - LM T
66 V/R2	LR SR, ANT POSN [FT, X.(R1, R2)]
67	LR VX, VY, VZ [FPS]
68	RNG(+Z), TG(BRK), VI [.1NM, M:S,.1FPS]
69 L	LS UPDT Z,Y,X (DN-R, XR, ALT) [FT]
70 L	AOTCODE(00YXX) [OCT(R1)] (XX=STAR ID Y=DTNT (Y=0 COAS/LPD CAL (P52 ONLY) (Y=1-6 AOT (L, F, R, RR, CL, LR) (Y=7 COAS
71 L	AOTCODE, X/CRSR, Y/SPRL CTR[OCT] (R1 SAME AS N70 EXCPT NO DTNT 0) (R2, R3 = POINTER:CTR (1-4 + LAST)
72	RR TRUN (⟶), SHFT (↕) [.01°(R1, R2)]
73 L	DSRD RR TRUN, SHFT [.01°(R1, R2)]
74	TFI, PITCHOVR Y, P [M:S, .01°, .01°]
75	P32: CDH ΔH,CSI/CDH ΔT,CDH/TPI ΔT P33: CDH ΔH, CDH/TPI ΔT, TPI SLIP [.1NM, M:S, M:S]
76 L	DSRD VHORZ(FNL), HDOT(FNL), XR [.1FPS, .1FPS, .1NM]
77	TCO, VGY(BODY), VI[M:S,.1FPS,.1FPS]
78	RR RNG, RNG RT(- CLOSE), TFI [.01NM, .1FPS, M:S]
79 L	CRSR, SPRL, DTNT [.01°, .01°, X.] (X=1-6 AOT-L, F, R, RR, CL, LR)
80	RR SEARCH DATA IND, LOS/+Z ∡ [XXXXX., .01°(R1, R2)] (+00000= SEARCH; +11111= LOCK)
81 L	ΔV(LV) VEC (FWD, RT, DN) [.1FPS]
82	CDH ΔV(LV) VEC (FWD,RT,DN)[.1FPS]
83	ΔV(BODY) VEC (UP, RT, FWD) [.1FPS]
84 L	ΔV(CSM LV) VEC (FWD,RT,DN)[.1FPS]
85	VG(BODY) VEC (UP, RT, FWD) [.1FPS]
86	N86 = N81
87 L	COAS AZ (+RT),EL (+ UP)[.01°(R1,R2)]
88	CELEST BODY UNIT VEC[.XXXXX]
89 L	LS LAT (+N), LON/2 (+E), ALT [.001°, .001°, .01NM]
90	Y, YDOT, PSI [.01NM, .1FPS, .01°] (Y, YDOT ⊥ CSM PL, PSI= LOS/LM PL)
91	ALT, VI, FLT PATH ∡ [10NM, FPS, .01°]
92	THRTL, HDOT (-/HI), H [%, .1FPS, FT]
93	Δ GYRO TORQ ∡ X, Y, Z [.001°]
94	VGX(BODY), HDOT (+/HI), H [.1FPS, FPS, FT]
99 L	W-MATRIX POSN, VEL, RR BIAS ERRS [FT, .1FPS, MILLI-RAD]

V50 CHECKLIST

R1	PLEASE PERFM	"PRO"	"E"
00013	CRS ALN	NORM	PLS TORQ
00014	ALN RECHK	RECHK	EXIT
00015	P51-ACQ STAR	CONT	CRS ALN
	P52 SPFY	PRO: PICAPAR, X/Y MK E: MAN SPFY, X/Y MK V32E: CRSR/SPRL MK;ROD BKUP	
00016	NOTE LGC REJ MK SETS (R2=REJ MK PRS)	CONT	REDO
00062	LGC PWR DN	CONT	
00201	RR SW - LGC	CONT	MAN ACQ (P20 ONLY)
00203	SW-PGNS/AUTO OR	CONT	MAN BURN
	SW-AUTO THRTL (PGNS/AUTO,) (NOT STAGED)	CONT	MAN THRTL
00205	CSM ACQUIRE	LOCK	ATT MNVR
00500	SW LR ANT TO POSN 1 (DES, WT 10, AUTO)	CONT	LR AT POSN 1

PGNS/AGS SUMMARY CARD

(LUMINARY 210/FP-8)
REV: 1   DATE: 6/3/71

Prepared for FPRB/MSC by TRW Systems
under Task ASPO 81C-3

Figure 5. Apollo 17 Verb and Noun List.

programmers with the basic naming structure for many of the various programs contained within the body of the AGC code that required interaction with the astronaut. Many of the major programs run by the AGC EXECUTIVE are numbered using two-digit codes.

Don Eyles contributed to the AGC code two routines formally named R11 and R13 that he informally called ROSENCRANTZ and GUILDENSTERN. These "names from Hamlet," he writes in his memoir, "swam into my consciousness because Tom Stoppard's *Rosencrantz and Guildenstern Are Dead* was then playing on Broadway."[8] The code introduces the R13 routine with three remarks cards, here transformed and remediated into contemporary Github-friendly formatted code:

```
#********************************************************************
# GUILDENSTERN:  AUTO-MODES MONITOR (R13)
#********************************************************************
```

The remarks continue:

HERE IS THE PHILOSOPHY OF GUILDENSTERN: ON EVERY APPEARANCE OR DISAPPEAR-
ANCE OF THE MANUAL THROTTLE DISCRETE TO SELECT P67 OR P66 RESPECTIVELY: ON
EVERY APPEARANCE OF THE ATTITUDE-HOLD DISCRETE TO SELECT P66 UNLESS THE
CURRENT PROGRAM IS P67 IN WHICH CASE THERE IS NO CHANGE.

These two routines, as Eyles explains, monitored switches and buttons; GUILDENSTERN, which was split into two lines as GUILDEN/STERN, the switch to manual mode and ROSENCRANTZ, buttons to abort landing.[9] The GUILDRET routine, riffing on GUILDENSTERN, was also added to this section of code. Eyles's comment addressing the way in which these two names "swam" into his consciousness demonstrates how the presence of natural language and arbitrarily named routines and programs links culture to code. The "philosophy of Guildenstern" became embedded within the code and, fittingly for Eyles's dramatic reference, this philosophy was attached to buttons that

https://authors.library.caltech.edu/5456/1/hrst.mit.edu/hrs/apollo/public/blairsmith2.htm.

8   Eyles, *Sunburst and Luminary*, 105.

9   There are no references to ROSENCRANTZ remaining within the Luminary099 code used in the Apollo 11 flight.

functioned to remove control from the computer and return it to a human, who might know better.

R00004

Cold War Code and
the Doubled Discourse of Programming

*"Does it change anything that Freud did not know
about the computer? And where should the moment of
suppression or of repression be situated in these new
models of recording and impression, or printing?"*
—Jacques Derrida, *Archive Fever*

The AGC code, as we have shown throughout this book, is an important archive of mid-twentieth-century computing culture. It speaks to us from this vital historical moment and comes to contemporary readers bearing traces of its moment of composition. The cultural work of this code is activated by the manipulation of a set of discourses that arises from the confluence of the languages, authors, and subject positions found operating within the code. The operation of the AGC depends on the co-existence of some of these discourses and the code explicitly provides the ability to mix modes of instruction as one of the main mechanisms. Other of these discourses circulating within the larger technological system are entirely external to the operation of the AGC. These include the Fordist division of labor that separated the distinct activities required to produce the AGC, the gendering of some of this labor, the partially implemented hierarchical management structures that organized the teams developing the code, and the code review and approval processes. Other discourses might instead be considered added on or supplemental — for example, the appearance of the non-functional referential wordplay found within the names of instructions and the code remarks. The operational logic of the AGC and these discourses participate in more than just computing culture, they also register larger patterns and processes of the modernizing project. As a final justification for the exploration and study of this now long obsolete and otherwise useless body of code, the recovery and interpretation of these discourses illuminate a crucial moment in the development of twentieth-century strategies of management and governing — of computers and people.

The Apollo Project and the associated developments that were produced within mid-century American computing were products of American Cold War culture. Audra J. Wolfe argues that "the relationships between science, technology, and national power built into the Apollo moon-landing program make it a quintessential Cold War phenomenon."[1] Similar techniques and systems were also heavily used by the U.S. military. Shortly after the Apollo 11 landing, beginning in the fall of 1969, large networks of sensors,

---

1 Audra J. Wolfe, *Competing with the Soviets: Science, Technology, and the State in Cold War America* (Baltimore: Johns Hopkins University Press, 2012), 89. See also Paul N. Edwards, *The Closed World: Computers and the Politics of Discourse in Cold War America* (Cambridge: MIT Press, 1996) and Stuart W. Leslie, *The Cold War and American Science: The Military-Industrial-Academic Complex at MIT and Stanford* (New York: Columbia University Press, 1993).

digital computers, and guided bombs, were deployed to Vietnam. These intelligent warfare systems were recommended by Harvard University and MIT faculty.[2] The majority of early artificial intelligence systems were all driven by military applications – from automated reconnaissance systems to automatons designed for hostile climates – for the war in Vietnam and were developed by researchers at MIT and Stanford University. These devices and methods, as Langdon Winner explains, have politics. For Winner, the automated reconnaissance systems would be examples of straightforward political technologies while the Apollo Project and the AGC in particular is an example of an inherently political technology, "man-made systems that appear to require, or to be strongly compatible with, particular kinds of political relationships."[3] Following Winner, we might think about certain software features within the AGC as appearing strongly compatible with contemporary strategies for the management and governing of people.

For the philosopher Gilles Deleuze, the middle of the twentieth century saw the demarcation of a new moment, a new epoch, in the administration of everyday life. Up until this point, from at least the middle of the nineteenth century, social life in the West was organized according to what Michel Foucault termed the disciplinary mode. For Deleuze, following Foucault, this mode of management was characterized by the centralized yet deeply internalized management of individuals that encouraged these people to conform themselves to the norms produced as they moved between various institutions or environments. Deleuze, in a short essay titled "Postscript on the Societies of Control," posits that the rapid modernization that followed World War II instituted a new set of practices organized around modulation and continuous change. He understands these new practices as operating in a control rather than disciplinary mode. "Control is short term and of rapid rates of turnover," Deleuze writes, "but also continuous and without limit, while discipline was of long duration, infinite and discontinuous."[4] The notion of this shift that still invokes a sense of centralized management but adds rapid yet continuous movements between sites of management – whereas before one was re-institutional-

2 Paul Dickinson provides an excellent account of the use of sensors in Vietnam, in particular those intended for use as part of what was called "McNamara's Line." See Paul Dickinson, *The Electronic Battlefield* (Bloomington: Indiana University Press, 1972).

3 Langdon Winner, "Do Artifacts Have Politics?" *Daedalus* 109, no. 1 (1980): 121–36, at 123.

4 Gilles Deleuze, "Postscript on the Societies of Control," *October* 59 (Winter 1992): 3–7, at 6.

ized, disciplined again, as one passed from site to site – doubles down on the already ongoing atomization of people and processes. Deleuze's concept of the control society borrows from the language of computing, suggesting that these metaphors and mechanisms have moved from hardware and software to governing practices. The implementation of control systems within computers, however, can serve as a site of dialectical exchange in which these technologies generate new metaphors and practices that may switch contexts from computers to culture but also the technologies themselves, through the work of the programmers and the administrators, take up and incorporate preexisting ideas and concepts, embedding them within their regular operation.

At the operational level, we can see several different ways in which the AGC implemented control over multiple discourses through the co-existence of multiple modes or methods of execution. The most important Basic/Yul instruction was TC, for Transfer Control. The TC instruction, like the colloquial "code switch" of language today, caused an immediate change from one set of instructions to another. To transfer control means to yield execution, although with the expectation that control will return. Deleuze's emphasis on the continuity of control finds as its analog the ceaselessness of computing, as processors cycle from instruction to instruction with each tick of the clock.

The concept of the interrupt, a core facility that enables the AGC's EXECUTIVE program to break execution of one job and run another job, illustrates how control mechanisms structure the movement between discourses within the code and within computing. The introduction of a capacity to cut short one line of execution and allow another to take priority provided a new way to handle complex events involving multiple demands on limited resources. Interruption was explicitly understood by the programmers as producing an intervention into the running program. It required a constantly running program, the EXECUTIVE, to serve as the AGC's traffic cop. This "master" control program makes decisions regarding the running of programs, although these are based on predetermined priorities, and thus interrupts can only be said to interrupt the execution of other programs, not the master discourse that structures the entire system. As each program runs, either to its proper conclusion or interrupted by another program, the EXECUTIVE maintains order over the program's access to limited computational resources.

The restricted syntax and difficulty of writing Basic/Yul instructions inspired the AGC programmers to add support for another more flexible language, one they called "Interpretive." In order to execute code written in Interpretive — this code all appeared within segments of Yul — control was transferred to the Interpretive program through the instruction TC INTPRET. Once control was transferred, the lines that followed up to an instruction EXIT that signaled the return back to Yul instructions were all executed by the Interpreter program. The co-existence of these two different languages is a special instance of transferring control within the AGC.

```
TC     INTPRET
VLOAD  ABVAL
VN1
STORE  ABVEL    # INITIALIZE ABVEL FOR P63 DISPLAY
EXIT
TCF    ENDOFJOB
```

The above lines co-mingle two programming languages and simultaneously produce a jump in execution from one to the other while preserving a continuous stream of instructions. The addition of Interpretive instructions adds new capacities to a limited language while preserving the AGC's larger control structures. This additional language, this additional discourse, works side by side with the original and primary language while other modes of discourse present within the code understand themselves as not stepping aside or subsumed by these methods but in some small way in opposition to them or at least registering their protest to pervasive and always-on control systems.

The earlier examples of the playful use of language included literary allusion and direct quotation. The programmers introduced some creativity into the names of various programs, constants, and subroutines. Leveraging the visual similarity between the zero character and the capital O, the programmers introduced a variation on the PXX program name structure to render P00 into POOH, which enabled them to add an entire universe of scatological references. The program is defined as such:

```
POOH    TC      RELDSP      # RELEASE DISPLAY SYSTEM

        CAF     PRIO5       # SET VARIABLE RESTART PRIORITY FOR
        TS      PHSPRDT2    # POO INTEGRATION.

        TC      CLRADMOD    # CLRADMOD DOES AN INHINT.

        CS      NODOBIT     # TURN OFF NODOFLAG.
        MASK    FLAGWRD2
        TS      FLAGWRD2

        CA      FIVE        # SET RESTART FOR STATEINT1
        TS      L
        COM
        DXCH    -PHASE2

        CS      OCT700      # TURN OFF P20, P25, IMU IN USE FLAG
        MASK    FLAGWRD0
        TS F    LAGWRD0     #               REMDFLG

        CAF     DNLADP00
```

The P00 is a Major Mode program and is part of the FRESH AND START RESTART section of the code. This program is responsible for resetting the system to a known state. The process of resetting the system involves cleaning or "flushing" stored data and thus the creation of several routines humorously known as MR.KLEAN, P00KLEAN, and ENEMA.[5]

```
MR.KLEAN    INHINT
            EXTEND
            DCA     NEG0
            DXCH    -PHASE2
    ...
```

5   A routine called KLEENEX was used to produce a virtual "cleaning" or wiping of anything currently appearing on the DSKY display: KLEENEX CLEANS OUT ALL MARK DISPLAYS (ACTIVE AND INACTIVE). A RETURN IS MADE TO THE USER AFTER THE MARK DISPLAYS.

```
POOKLEAN     EXTEND
             DCA    NEGO
             DXCH   -PHASE4

...
ENEMA  I     NHINT
             TC     STARTSB1
             TCF    GOPROG2A
```

These scatological references introduced into the code — users of the DSKY would never encounter any of these names — language that did not correspond to the norms of government computing. In turning P00 into a joke that was carried through to POOKLEAN and ENEMA, the programmers added levity to the serious project of the Space Race. These small jokes, like all successful jokes, were passed through the censors. The joke undercuts the force of the military-corporate-academic endeavor behind the scenes and undercover, but nevertheless still performs the required action.

The admixture of scatological language to the basic syntax of command-and-control culture corresponds to the roughly contemporary division between figures identified by Stewart Brand as the hackers and the planners. Brand is perhaps now best known for his desire to see satellite photography of the Earth: his widely distributed buttons that read "Why haven't we seen a photograph of the whole Earth yet?" Inspired by the photographs that were eventually released, Brand would go on to found the counter-cultural *Whole Earth Catalog,* a self-published catalog that first appeared in 1968 with a cover image of the Earth and advertised itself as providing "access to tools." Brand helped to introduce and decode computing culture to the public in "Spacewar: Fanatic Life and Symbolic Death Among the Computer Bums," his 1972 article for *Rolling Stone* on researchers working at California research laboratories, including the Stanford Artificial Intelligence (AI) Lab and Xerox PARC.[6] Brand understood there to be a cultural division at work in computing between those who considered themselves members of the counterculture - the heads, computer bums, and hackers - and those making use of computation to solve problems. One group was interested in the possibilities of computation as such and the

6   Stewart Brand, "Spacewar: Fanatic Life and Symbolic Death Among the Computer Bums,"
    Rolling Stone, December 7, 1972, 50–58.

other saw computers as a means to an end. Fred Turner glosses Brand's characterization of these earlier figures as the planners and the hackers:

> The planners were theoreticians, usually of the mind, who thought of computers as tools that could be used to generate or model information. The hackers focused on the computer systems themselves and on seeing what they could do. Within the lab, a culture clash emerged. Theory-oriented graduated students, equipped with well-funded and well-organized careers but not necessarily with computer programming expertise, resented the hackers' claims for computer time, as well as their free-wheeling style.[7]

The presence of the scatological language as an indicator of "freewheeling style" evinces perhaps some evidence of Brand's notion of the culture clash between these groups. The jokes are allowed to slip through, however, because they are ultimately inoffensive. The language remains suppressed, at one level, through the difference between code and instruction. While the natural language remarks cards and the remarks portion of the individual punch cards were ignored by the Yul System, the assembler would eventually convert everything into simple instructions for wiring the core memory of the AGC and reduce all language to mere signals, to 1s and 0s.

Early computing, nonetheless, had aspirations that participated in both the countercultural energy around the new possibilities found in these devices and those aspects of computing that were linked to ends including corporate development and military applications. We can see an example of these twinned desires in the material construction of Theodor H. Nelson's 1974 *Whole Earth Catalog*-inspired *Computer Lib/Dream Machines*. This self-consciously doubled text refuses synthesis and integration. Nelson writes of his rationale for creating a text with two sides, a book that presents itself to the reader with two faces, with two covers:

> This side of the book, *Computer Lib* proper (whose title is nevertheless the simplest way to refer to both halves), is an attempt to explain simply and concisely why computers are marvelous and wonderful, and what some main things are in the field. The second half of the book, *Dream Machines*, is specifically about fantasy and imagination, and new tech-

7   Fred Turner, *From Counterculture to Cyberculture: Stewart Brand, the Whole Earth Network, and the Rise of Digital Utopianism* (Chicago: University of Chicago Press, 2006), 133.

niques for it. That half is related to this half, but can be read first; I wanted to separate them as distinctly as possible.[8]

Nelson's division of the work of the imagination from explanation turns on the counter-cultural charge or frisson generated by the appropriation of computers for non-instrumental uses. In this moment right before the birth of the personal computer, such uses were mostly seen as wasteful and inappropriate.

In a 1971 article on computer programing and the Apollo Guidance Computer project written by Timothy Crouse and appearing in *Rolling Stone*, Don Eyles described himself as smoking marijuana on the job at MIT and being one of Charles Reich's "Consciousness-IIIers."[9] Working within what he calls "ye olde military industrial complex," Eyles presents himself as one of several counter-cultural figures, one of the "non-straight minority" deploying a minor language to write his way through the major language of government-funded academic technocrats. The command-and-control language of the Cold War, as mentioned earlier, saturates computer culture and the Apollo project. The Apollo project, as Crouse makes clear, existed alongside the majority military work of the rest of the Draper Lab: "Half of the Lab works full time on perfecting the Polaris and Poseidon missiles. Since its inception in 1939, the Lab has worked entirely on military projects. The one exception is the Apollo project."[10]

If the scatological references slid through the censors, the programmers needed the addition of a warning to accompany another creative use of language. Introducing a routine with the name or tag of BURNBABY, the authors and maintainers (explicitly identified in the code segment as ADLER AND EYLES) included a French phrase HONI SOIT QUI MAL Y PENSE, usually translated as "may he be shamed who thinks badly of it."[11] Eyles recalls that he was directing shame toward other readers of the code, those project managers who might disapprove of the "transgressive name [...] [an] allusion to the 1965 riots in the Watts section of Los Angeles. 'Burn, baby, burn' was

8   Theodor H. Nelson, *Computer Lib/Dream Machines* (Chicago: Theodor H. Nelson, 1974).

9   Timothy Crouse, "Don Eyles: Extra! Weird-Looking Freak Saves Apollo 14!" *Rolling Stone*, March 18, 1971, https://www.rollingstone.com/politics/politics-news/don-eyles-extra-weird-looking-freak-saves-apollo-14-40737/.

10   Ibid., 6.

11   *Oxford English Dictionary*, s.v. "honi soit qui mal y pense."

shouted by the rioters as they set fire to looted storefronts."[12] The programmers introduced this phrase to transgress the line between the two cultures of computing. BURNBABY provides a particularly compelling example of the movement of language from culture to code and back into popular culture, and the term "burn" for firing an engine, Eyles explains, became "deeply embedded" and is now fully a part of the language.

In Timothy Crouse's article, Don Eyles offered up the following understanding of the frustrations he experienced as a result of the limited audience available for the text that he was writing:

> Eyles and some of his fellow Consciousness IIIers regard computer programming as a fine craft that might some day be elevated to the status of an art. "It's possible to envision a time when there are professors of the literature of computer programming. Maybe some programmers will be minor poets of the 20th Century. The trouble is that programs are written in a language there's no audience for. It's like Nabokov's book about Gogol where at the end he says that if you really want to know anything about Gogol, there's no way around it, you gotta learn Russian. It's sort of discouraging."[13]

In his memoir, Eyles writes of his desire that his book might help revise the "foundation myth of the contemporary digital culture" and inspire not "the next internet startups or the next social medium" but "idealistic planetary goals. Exploring others. Sustaining this one."[14] He recognizes the extent to which corporate culture has found it easy to appropriate the idealism of early computing and to turn the enthusiasm of developers like himself into the drive for creating profitable technologies. Digital culture has always been marked by twin impulses: one a little anarchic and the other a bit more corporate. Cyberlibertarian discourses attempt to synthesize these, but perhaps we can find other ways to build a usable past from computing history.

One way might be to turn to the resource of the suppressed language found in code as a source for poetic language. We can do so by means of a bit

12 Eyles, *Sunburst and Luminary*, 96.
13 Crouse, "Don Eyles," 6.
14 Eyles, *Sunburst and Luminary*, xviii.

of a deconstruction of the binary that for the philosopher Martin Heidegger structures the difference between what he terms traditional and technological language. This strategy might help us not just understand the purpose of the AGC, but free the many possible meanings of the AGC code. For Heidegger, the difference between technological and traditional rests in the capacity of what he calls the "mystery" of traditional language to conceal "the unspoken and what is inexpressible." We understand the natural language appearing in source code to be a variety of traditional language, much like poetic language, complete with all the attributes and problems of expression. "The handing down in tradition is not a mere passing on," he writes, "it is the preservation of what is original, it is the safeguarding of the new possibilities of the already spoken language."[15] He argues that "the handing down in the tradition of a language is realized through the language itself, and indeed in such a way that, for this, it lays claim to the human being to say the world anew from the language that is preserved and thus to bring what is not-yet-seen into appearance."[16] Technological language, on the other hand — and the instruction-laden discourse of computer code, which would seem to be technological language in its ideal form — is dominated by a drive for communication, the clarification of a sequence of signs. Rather than just assigning the free form natural language of the "Remarks" recorded in the AGC code to the traditional and the instructions themselves as technological language, we want to frame the entire text as possessing a wealth of opportunities — resources for bringing the not-yet-seen into language. Code, as this book demonstrates, has poetic possibilities. This technological artifact is truly world changing. Not just functional, not just historical, the AGC code is alive with a captivating language that pulls us into an altered relation with possibility as such. Flipping the moonbit reorients us. In an instant, our coordinate system has changed and we have displaced our center and made the Earth a little uncanny.

Exceeding mere function and communication, the Apollo Guidance Computer code deploys a whole world of traditional and technological language — scatological, comical, literary, self-referential, machinic, and more —

15   Martin Heidegger, "Traditional Language and Technological Language," trans. Wanda Torres Gregory, *The Journal of Philosophical Research* 23 (1998): 129–45, at 142.
16   Ibid.

to give poets and readers the resources to use this body of code to say the world, nay, the universe, anew.

Bibliography

Alonso, Ramon, J. Halcombe Laning, Jr., and Hugh Blair-Smith.
   E-1077: Preliminary MOD 3C Programmers Manual. Cambridge: MIT
   Instrumentation Laboratory, 1961.

Barry, John A. *Technobabble.* Cambridge: MIT Press, 1991.

Berry, David M. *The Philosophy of Software Code and Mediation in the
   Digital Age.* New York: Palgrave, 2011.

Bervin, Jen. *Nets.* Brooklyn: Ugly Duckling Presse, 2004.

Blair-Smith, Hugh. "Annotations to Eldon Hall's *Journey to the Moon*."
   Apollo Guidance Computer History Project, February 1997. https://
   authors.library.caltech.edu/5456/1/hrst.mit.edu/hrs/apollo/public/
   blairsmith.htm.

Bolter, Jay David, and Richard Grusin. *Remediation: Understanding New
   Media.* Cambridge: MIT Press, 1999.

Borsuk, Amaranth, Jesper Juul, and Nick Montfort. "Opening a Worl in
   the World Wide Web: The Aesthetics and Poetics of Deletionism." *NMC:
   Media-N* 11, no. 1 (2015). http://median.newmediacaucus.org/the_
   aesthetics_of_erasure/opening-a-worl-in-the-world-wide-web-the-
   aesthetics-and-poetics-of-deletionism/.

Brand, Stewart. "Spacewar: Fanatic Life and Symbolic Death Among the
   Computer Bums." *Rolling Stone,* December 7, 1972, 50–58.

Cayley, John. "The Code Is Not the Text (Unless It Is the Text)." *Electronic
   Book Review,* September 10, 2002. http://www.electronicbookreview.
   com/thread/electropoetics/literal.

Chun, Wendy Hui Kyong. *Programmed Visions: Software and Memory.*
   Cambridge: MIT Press, 2011.

"Computers in Spaceflight: The NASA Experience." *NASA.* https://history.
   nasa.gov/computers/Ch2-5.html.

Cook, William W. "Writing in the Spaces Left." *College Composition and
   Communication* 44, no. 1 (1993): 9–25. DOI: 10.2307/358481.

Crouse, Timothy. "Don Eyles: Extra! Weird-Looking Freak Saves Apollo
   14!" *Rolling Stone,* March 18, 1971. https://www.rollingstone.com/
   politics/politics-news/don-eyles-extra-weird-looking-freak-saves-
   apollo-14-40737.

Deleuze, Gilles. "Postscript on the Societies of Control." *October* 59 (Winter 1992): 3-7. https://www.jstor.org/stable/778828.

Derrida, Jacques. *Archive Fever: A Freudian Impression.* Translated by Eric Prenowitz. Chicago: University of Chicago Press, 1995.

Dickinson, Paul. *The Electronic Battlefield.* Bloomington: Indiana University Press, 1972.

"Different Programming Styles." *Apollo Guidance Computer History Project: Second Conference,* September 14, 2001. https://authors.library.caltech.edu/5456/1/hrst.mit.edu/hrs/apollo/public/conference2/styles.htm.

Dobson, James E. *Critical Digital Humanities: The Search for a Methodology.* Urbana: University of Illinois Press, 2019.

Edwards, Paul N. *The Closed World: Computers and the Politics of Discourse in Cold War America.* Cambridge: MIT Press, 1996.

Eyles, Don. *Sunburst and Luminary: An Apollo Memoir.* Boston: Fort Point Press, 2018.

Fisher, Ronald A. "The Use of Multiple Measurements in Taxonomic Problems." *Annals of Eugenics* 7 (1936): 179–88. DOI: 10.1111/j.1469-1809.1936.tb02137.x.

Galloway, Alexander R. *Protocol: How Control Exists after Decentralization.* Cambridge: MIT Press, 2004.

Hayles, N. Katherine. *How We Think: Digital Media and Contemporary Technogenesis.* Chicago: University of Chicago Press, 2012.

———. *My Mother Was a Computer: Digital Subjects and Literary Texts.* Chicago: University of Chicago Press, 2005.

Heidegger, Martin. "Traditional Language and Technological Language." Translated by Wanda Torres Gregory. *The Journal of Philosophical Research* 23 (1998): 129–45. DOI: 10.5840/jpr_1998_16.

Hunt, Amy. "Not Your Typical Prose: Documenting Software." MALS thesis, Dartmouth College, 2016.

"Innovations in Software." *Apollo Guidance Computer History Project: Second Conference,* September 14, 2001. https://authors.library.caltech.edu/5456/1/hrst.mit.edu/hrs/apollo/public/conference2/innovations.htm.

Kittler, Friedrich A. *The Truth of the Technological World: Essays on the Genealogy of Presence.* Translated by Erik Butler. Stanford: Stanford University Press, 2014.

Knuth, Donald. "Literate Programming." *The Computer Journal* 27, no. 2 (1984): 97–111. DOI: 10.1093/comjnl/27.2.97.

Lee Shetterly, Margot. *Hidden Figures: The American Dream and the Untold Story of the Black Women Who Helped Win the Space Race*. New York: William Morrow and Company, 2016.

Leslie, Stuart W. *The Cold War and American Science: The Military-Industrial-Academic Complex at MIT and Stanford*. New York: Columbia University Press, 1993.

Levine, Caroline. *Forms: Whole, Rhythm, Hierarchy, Network*. Princeton: Princeton University Press, 2015.

Mackenzie, Adrian. *Machine Learners: Archaeology of a Data Practice*. Cambridge: MIT Press, 2017.

Manovich, Lev. *Software Takes Command*. New York: Bloomsbury, 2013.

Marino, Mark C. "Why We Must Read the Code: The Science Wars, Episode IV." In *Debates in the Digital Humanities*, edited by Matthew K. Gold and Lauren F. Klein, 139–52. Minneapolis: University of Minnesota Press, 2016.

Mawler, Stuart. "Executable Texts: Programs as Communications Devices and Their Use in Shaping High-tech Culture." MSc thesis, Virginia Polytechnic Institute and State University, 2007. http://hdl.handle.net/10919/31388.

McHale, Brian. "Poetry under Erasure." In *Theory Into Poetry: New Approaches to the Lyric*, edited by Eva Müller-Zettelmann and Margarete Rubik, 277–301. New York: Rodopi, 2005.

Montfort, Nick, Patsy Baudoin, John Bell, Ian Bogost, Jeremy Douglass, Mark C. Marino, Michael Mateas, Casey Reas, Mark Sample, and Noah Vawter. *10 PRINT CHR$(205.5+RND(1)); : GOTO 10*. Cambridge: MIT Press, 2013.

Morash, Russell, dir. *Computer for Apollo*. Cambridge: MIT Science Reporter, 1965.

Nakamura, Lisa. "Indigenous Circuits: Navajo Women and the Racialization of Early Electronic Manufacture." *American Quarterly* 66, no. 4 (2014): 919–41. DOI: 10.1353/aq.2014.0070.

Nelson, Theodor H. *Computer Lib/Dream Machines*. Chicago: Theodor H. Nelson, 1974.

O'Brien, Frank. *The Apollo Guidance Computer: Architecture and Operation*. Chichester: Springer, 2010.

Office of the Press Secretary, "President Obama Names Recipients of the Presidential Medal of Freedom." *The White House*, November 16, 2016. https://obamawhitehouse.archives.gov/the-press-office/2016/11/16/president-obama-names-recipients-presidential-medal-freedom.

Philip, M. NourbeSe. *Zong!* Middletown: Wesleyan University Press, 2011.

Phillips, Tom. *A Humument.* London: Thames and Hudson, 1980.

Raley, Rita. "Code.surface ‖ Code.depth." *Dichtung Digital* 36 (2006). http://www.dichtung-digital.org/2006/1-Raley.htm

Tenen, Dennis. *Plain Text: The Poetics of Computation.* Stanford: Stanford University Press, 2017.

Turner, Fred. *From Counterculture to Cyberculture: Stewart Brand, the Whole Earth Network, and the Rise of Digital Utopianism.* Chicago: University of Chicago Press, 2006.

Ullman, Ellen. *Life in Code.* New York: Farrar, Straus and Giroux, 2017.

Unsworth, John. "New Methods for Humanities Research." http://people.virginia.edu/~jmu2m/lyman.htm

Winner, Langdon. "Do Artifacts Have Politics?" *Daedalus* 109, no. 1 (1980): 121–36. https://www.jstor.org/stable/20024652.

Wolfe, Audra J. *Competing with the Soviets: Science, Technology, and the State in Cold War America.* Baltimore: Johns Hopkins University Press, 2012.

Made in the USA
Middletown, DE
02 November 2019

77869897R00084